D1527131

THE
FAMILY
UNCONSCIOUS

Cover art by *Jane A. Evans*

THE FAMILY UNCONSCIOUS
"An invisible bond"

E. BRUCE TAUB-BYNUM

*This publication made possible with
the assistance of the Kern Foundation*

THE THEOSOPHICAL PUBLISHING HOUSE
Wheaton, Ill. U.S.A. / Madras, India / London, England

For additional information write to:

The Theosophical Publishing House, 306 West Geneva Road, Wheaton, Illinois 60189. Published by the Theosophical Publishing House, a department of the Theosophical Society in America.

Library of Congress Cataloging in Publication Data

Taub-Bynum, E. Bruce (Edward Bruce), 1948-
   The family unconscious.

   (Quest book)
   "A Quest original."
   Includes bibliographical references and index.
   1. Subconsciousness.   2. Family.   3. Jung, C.G.
   (Carl Gustav), 1875-1961.   I. Title.
BF315.T35   1984   150.19'5   83-40237
ISBN 0-8356-0582-5   (pbk.)

Printed in the United States of America

To my beloved wife Alyse
who helps and then helps even more;

to my family, whose matrix expands, enfolds;

to Ernie, Jake, Don and
Kent, whose friendship and vision
is beyond estimate or event;

to William and Bennett for the good times;

to the voices of my Sadhana
I no longer ignore;

to my guides on the inner journey,
Sri Swami Rama and Sri Swami Muktananda;

to all those of the "sixties generation"
who have not yet forgotten that mind
once opened and arched beyond itself.

Contents

Foreword by Stanley Krippner, ix

Introduction, xiii

Section I   The Enfolding Field

       1 The Family's Shared Field, 3

       2 Related Phenomena, 15

Section II   Family Dreams

       3 The Dreaming Night and the Clinical Office, 27

       4 Family Dreamwork, 35

Section III   The Radiant Organism

       5 Energy Systems of the Body, Yoga, and Biofeedback, 43

       6 The Autonomic Nervous System and The Science of Breath, 53

Section IV   Psi, Dreams, and the Family Unconscious

       7 The Sinew of Consciousness, 63

       8 Dreams, Energy Systems, and Family Life, 73

       9 The Anatomy of Sleep, 82

       10 Information and Transformation, 94

       11 Chakras and Affective Currents, 100

       12 Chakras and Family Motifs, 107

13 The Family Unconscious in Day-to-Day Life, 114

Section V Toward a New Paradigm: Psi, Physics, Psychology, and the Self

14 Psychology and the New Physics, 125

15 Interconnections: Information and Energy, 138

16 Ego, Duality, and Perception, 148

17 Neurology and Consciousness, 159

18 The Self and Perception, 170

19 The Self, Energy, and the Roots of Transcendence, 182

Section VI The Common Stream

20 Family Life and Healing, 195

Epilogue, 203

Appendix A The Biological Aspects of Psi Plasma, 207

Appendix B Four Types of Interaction, 209

Notes, 210

Glossary, 225

Index, 227

Foreword
Stanley Krippner

Family theory is a growth-oriented approach that focuses on the problems of individuals in the context of their family system. Behavior change is not aimed at the individual but at the family system, which includes each member's thoughts, beliefs, and interpersonal connections processed in a variety of patterns. Nathan Ackerman (1971), a pioneer in this field, observed that in family therapy, "The concept of mental disorder is expanded to a constellation of multiple vulnerabilities, now afflicting one member, now another. These disturbances are interdependent and interpenetrating.... To save any one member, we must mobilize the healing power of the whole family" (p. 152).

Edward Bruce Taub-Bynum has written eloquently about his firsthand experiences as a family therapist, and about the "enfolding field" of the "family unconscious." In so doing, he echoes the observation of Don Jackson (1968), one of the earliest family therapists, who conceptualized the family as a closed system in which "variations in output or behavior are fed back in order to correct the system's response" (p. 2). The importance of communicative behaviors is emphasized by Jackson; these communications, according to Taub-Bynum, often exist at levels beneath conscious awareness, yet influence family members in profound and often unexpected ways.

How can we account for the extraordinary forms of communication among family members reported by Taub-Bynum? Assuming that the instances are accurate and occur too frequently to be coincidental, we are left with the hypotheses of extended sensory perception and extra-sensory perception. In the former, messages are carried subliminally through eye movements, shifts in posture, intonation of speech, and other forms of nonverbal communication and body language. In the latter, information is passed from one family member to another in ways that seem to circumvent our ordinary constructs of time and space. We use such terms as *telepathy* and *ESP* to refer to these incidents, but have no satisfactory explanation of them (Krippner, 1984).

Taub-Bynum attempts to place these data within the rubrics which are available in quantum-relativistic theory. For years psychology has been criticized for slavishly modelling itself after the physical sciences. Yet, it must continue to do so. One can envision a quantum-age psychology which allows room for the relativistic, the indeterminable, and the absence of strict divisions between the observer and the observed. There are lessons here for family therapy, and Taub-Bynum has identified several for us.

The field of family therapy has developed quite rapidly over the past few decades. The family therapist typically perceives the family as a system (i.e., any complex of elements in mutual interaction) that passes through a series of developmental stages. Taub-Bynum describes the family unconscious in developmental terms, the result of recurrent transactional patterns. He also describes it as a system which is influenced by each family member.

The author illustrates his concept with material drawn from actual family-therapy sessions. In so doing, he conveys the richness of shared imagery and emotionality that operates in the life of each family member. Dreams, of course, are a splendid source of data, and seem to be the most direct route the therapist may take to explore the family unconscious. The author also uses yoga as a resource for both theory and therapy, grounding it in physiology to prevent the discussion from becoming unduly esoteric.

The Family Unconscious is a creative effort, and like many provocative books it will arouse controversy. I would urge the reader to focus upon practical implications of Taub-Bynum's ideas. Of course there will be disagreements in some quarters with certain aspects of his conceptual scheme. Nevertheless, the "enfolding field" described in these pages may provide a route of mending and healing for many families who are denizens of our tattered social fabric. If the family is the unit of society, we ignore its present pressures and crises at our own peril.

REFERENCES

Ackerman, N. *The psychodynamics of family life: Diagnosis and treatment of family relationships.* New York: Basic Books, 1958.

Jackson, D. The question of family homeostasis. In D. Jackson (Ed.), *Communication, family and marriage.* Palo Alto, CA: Science & Behavior Books, 1968.

Krippner, S. (Ed.) *Advances in parapsychological research* (Vol. 4). Greensboro, NC: McFarland, 1984.

Introduction

There is a great romance going on today between the modern mind and science. Like every romance, it is infused with a sense of limitless energy, feeling, and intuition. Also, like every great affair, it is always in danger of error and overestimation by the partners. One child of this marriage in the nuclear bedroom is a new vision of wholeness and interconnection emerging from physics. Its twin is the nightmare of thermonuclear war. For the first time in the history of our species, we live each day on the verge of eternity. Science, for good or ill, is no longer isolated from our day-to-day lives. It reaches into the most intimate of cloisters, family life itself.

This book touches that aspect of our common psychology that interfaces us with all. The family network of feelings, images, and energy emerges is a powerful system we term the Family Unconscious. This web touches and enfolds us each day, each night, its energy and affect a vital function of our personal lives. The science of consciousness has reached into our innermost hearts, the roots of the dream, the deepest of emotional connections, and our primary values. On this most intimate of levels science has revealed a certain interconnectedness in shared feelings or dreams which parallels the interconnection of subatomic particles. This book is written with this central theme in mind.

Whether we believe that man is a fallen angel or a risen ape, we all find ourselves in a similar situation, although with differing perspectives. The stupendous achievements of the contemporary mechanistic model for science and society for over two centuries have brought wealth to certain areas of the world. But also in the process they have created a dangerous and unprecedented crisis. This is a crisis not only for one or two nations but for all nations and peoples on the planet. It encompasses not only the economic orders, including capitalist, socialist, and Communist, but also the spectacular web of poverty, wealth, weapons, and nearly instantaneous communication in the "global village."

This crisis in the final decades of the twentieth century witnesses us hurling through vast paradigmatic shifts. Our changing scientific and philosophical world views, an inextricable aspect of this kaleidoscopic situation, are reflecting more and more interconnections. At the other pole of our consciousness, the Family Unconscious expresses that most intimate field of shared feeling, imagery, and emotional energy that touches our seemingly separate personalities, dreamlife, and unusual channels of communication, enfolding us all in a common tongue.

In the scientific community, that vital subsystem of our shared human endeavor, there is underway a revolution of immense impact on both our global and intimate lives. It is a perspective that encompasses not only the field of matter and energy but recently also consciousness itself. Both of these are coming to be regarded as interpenetrating aspects of the universe. Across the whole spectrum of inquiry, the eye of modern science has come to focus more and more on the emergence of systems of self-organization and on the enfolding web of functions and events. Systems of increasing complexity are emerging that defy earlier concepts of entropy, not only on the chemical but also on the biochemical level, and ultimately the level of highly complex organisms that result in self-consciousness, ourselves.

It appears that self-organization and self-regulation are realized on each plane of human inquiry and experience. We know that we can direct our consciousness on different levels—the interpersonal, organic, biochemical, physiological—by way of psychosomatic processes and biofeedback procedures, and thus affect our bodily functions. In the "other direction" we have begun to see the emergence of self-organizing properties "below" the chemical level in the domain of atomic and subatomic events. Self-organization and field behavior on the subquantum and quantum levels affect self-organization on the chemical level, which influences processes on the biochemical level, which interfaces with our self-conscious level. Many people are coming to feel that along this whole continuum, matter, meaning, and intentionality are co-extensive. The "self" of "self-organizing principles" appears to pervade all the planes of knowledge. This is certainly the case with the "self" in the system of the Family Unconscious. The universe of matter, energy, and consciousness is emerging as an undivided whole from both scientific theory and intimate personal experience.

This book explores and hopefully offers a penumbral illumination of this perspective for us as individuals as well as collectively. In the vast "spectrum of consciousness," we are focusing on the biosocial and transpersonal bandwidths. We hope to see how energy and consciousness operate in these systems and therein move further from fragmentation to wholeness, from bits in separation to union or yoga. To this end we introduce in the first section the roots and operation of the Family Unconscious.

In the second and third sections the emergence of personally shared affect, energy, and dreamscape along with psi material and clinical phenomena will be presented. This is done in order to flesh out our presentation with data which the reader may examine in the light of his or her own immediate life and experience. We will draw much from practice in biofeedback, hypnosis, and the field of family therapy.

The fourth section will focus on experience and theory as a basis for the operation of psi and will draw heavily from clinical observation, research, and the realm of the new physics. None of these phenomena are isolated from day-to-day life. Each chapter will reflect in a specific way how the Family Unconscious operates in reference to a specific area. In this context, it will be quite natural to bring back from modern scientific repression those formative and teleological causative influences to join the material and efficient causes so that, as with Aristotle, we have a fully functioning science.

Various scientific theories will be used to highlight events and processes in the journey we will take. However, we want to state clearly that these scientific theories and findings are guideposts, not the final word in these matters. They are helpful and suggestive, but the territory is not the map.

The fifth section will seek an integration of the previous material with those principles of field and self-organization that have emerged over the whole range of the new science. We will explore the implications of all this for us. Here we will go deeply into contemporary science and draw helpful but limited parallels to these principles as we see them operating through the Family Unconscious. The main thrust will be to demonstrate the undivided wholeness of both the field of matter and energy, and of the vast enfolding field of consciousness. At a certain level both of these go trans-temporal and trans-spatial. This becomes apparent not only in unusual experiences, but also in the heart of everyday matters.

The final section will return to our day-to-day life where all these principles are rooted, the family. Here the direction of modern science and the vision of the ancient Rishis of India may be seen to merge and prepare us for the next stage in the evolution of our species.

I

The Enfolding
Field

There probably exists in the mental life of the individual not only what he has experienced himself, but also what he brought with him at birth, fragments of phylogenetic origin, an archaic heritage . . . . The archaic heritage of mankind includes not only dispositions, but also ideational contents, memory traces of the experiences of former generations.

Freud, Moses and Monotheism

In addition to our immediate consciousness, which is of a thoroughly personal nature and which we believe to be the only empirical psyche (even if we tack on the personal unconscious as an appendix), there exists a second psychic system of a collective, universal and impersonal nature which is identical in all individuals. This collective unconscious does not develop individually, but is inherited. It consists of preexistent forms, the archetypes, which can only become conscious secondarily and which give definite form to certain psychic contents.

Jung, Archetypes and the Collective Unconscious

. . . specific morphogenetic fields are responsible for the characteristic form and organization of systems at all levels of complexity, not only in the realm of biology, but also in the realm of chemistry and physics. These fields order the systems with which they are associated by affecting events which, from an energetic point of view, appear to be indeterminate or probabilistic . . . morphogenetic fields of all past systems become present to any subsequent similar system; the structures of past systems affect subsequent similar systems by a cumulative influence which acts across both space and time.

R. Sheldrake, A New Science of Life

1

The Family's Shared Field

I tell you that I have a long way to go before
I am where one begins.
R. M. Rilke, Letter to a friend

For several nights she was repeatedly assaulted by vivid
dreams. In each dream family figures loomed up in odd and
familiar places. In one dream, which occurred on a Tuesday
night, two Chinese individuals led a procession of mourners
to her front door. They called her "Mrs. Jefferson" and said
how sad they were. For complicated reasons this woman,
now living several states away from her parents, had not
really spoken with them for a number of years. A few days
after the dream her sister called and informed her that their
parents had just had the "unveiling" of her brother's tomb-
stone. This is a Jewish custom in which a ceremony is held
on the anniversary of a death. The brother had died in an
auto accident a year and three months earlier, so the unveiling was three months late. While at the family home
with the mourners, the parents were emotionally very intense, the mother even passing out. The dreamer was
totally unaware that the unveiling had been postponed for
three months. The unveiling was held on the same Tuesday
as the dream. The deceased brother had had two significant

romances with Chinese women in his life, and his name was Jeffrey !

It seems this dreamer had somehow unconsciously touched upon a deep, collective image or bed of information. She seemed to have a particular skew on an idea and emotional information field that all members of the family shared. The family system really appeared to be a whole.

I had always been curious about this kind of phenomena, but I did not really explore it until the year of my post-doctoral fellowship at a small, family therapy oriented hospital. After full sessions with families where all were present, we would work with parts or subsystems of the family. Often in these situations with siblings or parents "family secrets" would emerge. When the timing was right for these secrets to come out to the whole family, somehow everyone seemed to already have a vague image of the other's secret, even though these had never been openly mentioned. Such secrets often included the oddest of acts and the most intimate of fantasies. There seemed to be a shared central image, not fully located in any one person, but with each member having his or her own perception of it. I assumed that there must have been some nonverbal communication going on. Yet this did not completely account for other similar observations I had made in family therapy. All this stretched to the limits my fledgling models of family process, including the psychodynamic and systems ones, but I still felt relatively new to the field and so assumed I'd gradually learn.

Many family therapy cases involved problems that were openly present in one generation, skipped the next wave or generation, only to reappear in the third generation. These often involved character problems and drug or other substance abuse. Available models described how a symptom, never spoken of, could disappear then reemerge a generation or more later, but they could not explain this to my satisfaction. Somehow in situations like this time and space were handled differently from what I would have expected. I knew that there is no time in the unconscious, but I experienced extreme difficulty seeing space as something with no "location." Then one day a whole new phenomenological circus came to town.

We began treating one family in which the parents were in the midst of a separation. One of the central issues was the mother's "overinvolvement" with her nine-year-old son, Matt. When we explored this "overinvolvement," we found that it consisted of a claim by mother and son to be able to read each other's minds at times. I had heard of this phenomena and seen it briefly in hospitalized patients who were decompensating, i.e., having a mental breakdown. It is termed "psychotic insight." However, no one in this family appeared to be in that category. I asked the family about this phenomenon, and they produced a number of detailed examples. Again I questioned the limits of available models.

It began to dawn on me that some new notion of individuality and boundary was nestling here. The "boundaries" of individuals were being forced into different constellations. I had found many times that, though a particular problem was not spoken of in a family, nevertheless one family member somehow expressed the pain of another member. Several times the initial insight into a problem had come by way of a family member's dream. The spread and enfolding of the shared emotion I had often witnessed also reinforced this idea of wholeness and interconnection looming before me.

Eventually it occurred to me that emotions, even when strongly felt in an area of the body, are not in any one location as objects are in a specific location. I saw that the "transmission" of these emotions did not have to obey strict laws of physics. This opened a door for me which I then asked others to consider.

My supervisor dismissed this as all nonsense, including the uncanny events in the "overinvolvement" situation. He playfully asked me about my own state of mind. However, the "data" kept appearing. Finally I decided to ask some families to keep records of their dreams. My reasoning was that dreams as unconscious productions of the psyche might reveal some systems-wide unconscious process. (Dreams will be explored in the next section.) To my intellectual surprise, but intuitive acknowledgment, these dreams turned out to reveal innumerable interconnections of affects, images, and ideas and showed crosscurrents of unconscious systems influencing family members.

By now I had collected a considerable number of incidents in which information within a family system seemed to spread without overt communication, not only across generations, but also across space and time, sometimes through dreams. It seemed to me that, in addition to a personal or individual unconscious and a collective unconscious, there was another active, dynamic level of consciousness that deeply influences our thoughts, emotions, and psychic energy. This affective energy level thrives in the powerful network of family patterns and emerges as the Family Unconscious.

Eventually my colleagues began to tell me of their own "curious" situations that involved such processes. I began to look deeper into these space-and-time anomalies and to accept that this process of information exchange is a real and valid area of study, despite the current professional and scientific prejudice against such phenomena. My acceptance was strengthened as I increased my knowledge of that part of the professional and folk literature, both ancient and modern, which explores the area.

As you read through these pages you will come to see situations and episodes that are similar to your own experiences, whether unusual occurrences in dreams, family situations, "crisis telepathy" which we will look at later, or beyond. Before that, however, we must put this whole area on firm observational and theoretical ground. Each chapter of this book will seek to do just that in its own way, with each section coming back to the central theme of the Family Unconscious and its manifold expressions.

ROOTS OF THE FIELD

Dreams bring together, transmute, and symbolize elements from various areas of our life. Figures of people and snatches of events might come from everyday life experiences or emerge from scenarios experienced long ago. The feeling tone might be one of which we are barely aware and cannot express in our waking life. It may be vivid and powerful with emotional meaning and impact which is inexpressible in words. Symbols and images often emerge from layers of consciousness not available at all in our ordinary waking state. The Family Unconscious as a vortex and shared field of feeling spans all these.

The nonlogical and intensely symbolic part of the dreamwork process, and also some waking states, are called by psychologists *primary process*. The Family Unconscious functions in a way that integrates various aspects and areas of data and commonsense observations into a coherent, viable system, a system that includes the primary process level of the psyche. Our journey will explore the system of the Family Unconscious in detail and will demonstrate how it operates and interfaces with other systems of consciousness, including the primary process levels. We will also present a number of clinical examples of how it manifests in our psychological and psychic experience.

Modern psychology has accepted for some time the working hypothesis of an unconscious part of the mind. (1,2) Indeed, the discovery of the unconscious and its systematic exploration at the beginning of the twentieth century was one of the greatest findings of the emerging Western science of consciousness. The web of conflicts, defense mechanisms, and internecine motivations and events demonstrated to these explorers at that time that the unconscious was not only a daily reality of human functioning, but also that it had a place in science as an empirically developed concept. They looked at their own experiences, as you the reader are asked to do, in order to see from where they spring.

For Freud this unconscious was empirically derived. It is a region of the psyche containing materials that were once conscious but later became the prisoners of repression. This dark inner landscape was inhabited, not only by memories of a prohibitive nature to the conscious mind, but also—and this is very important—by sensory and motor experience. We are unaware of many impressions coming in from our senses and from muscle movements. However, these are registered by the part of our nervous system that works without conscious direction, the autonomic nervous system. Thus these impressions are outside or beyond waking consciousness. They do, however, reflect our mental and emotional "intentions." The range and subtlety of our intentionality is therefore vast and intricate and interfaces with the most intimate aspects of our material nature.

Although different theories and languages are used to define the energies and dynamics of the unconscious, it is generally understood to be the outcome of our habitual ways of relating with significant others in our lives. These are termed by psychologists recurrent transactional patterns, and they deeply influence the way we handle all subjective experiences. Traumatic events are also registered here in our annals of personal history and metaphor. In the familiar topographical model of consciousness, it is the region of the psychie "below" the conscious mind and "deeper" than the other structure of this model termed the *preconscious*. The dreams of every one of us are rooted here, and these dreams are the royal road into the hinterland of the unconscious.

Carl Jung (3,4,) was the first Western psychologist to advance an operational concept of the collective unconscious. Jung held that the collective unconscious, in contrast to the Freudian unconscious, is an *inherited* faculty of the psyche and is not empirically developed. There were others in the West who had produced concepts similar to this. These included Levy-Bruhl's "primitive representation collectives," and from the study of comparative religion came the "categories of imagination" by Herbert and Moss. Add to this the idea of the "primordial thought" of Adolph Bastian, and we see that the intuition of the collective unconscious found expression through several explorers. Jung repeatedly cited the above in his work, along with his own "uncanny experiences" with the collective unconscious.

Jung's best known experience of this kind occurred while a woman client was relating her dream of an ancient Egyptian scarab. At that very moment an insect flew into Jung's window, one which looked exactly like the insect the woman was describing in her dream! The insect was not only very uncommon in that part of the world, but it was also the wrong season for it to appear. Another such event involved a conversation between Jung and Freud in Jung's office in which Jung advanced the idea of psychic influences on the material world. Freud asserted that it was "all garbage." At that instant in Jung's office a loud noise out of nowhere announced the unexplained breaking of an artifact on the mantle. Freud proceeded to faint, and Jung picked up the father of psychoanalysis and took him out of the room. Jung called this particular kind of event *synchronicity.*

The collective unconscious in all Jung's works was seen as the inherited thought patterns that result from thousands and thousands of years of human interaction around specific roles, situations, and themes. These appear in dreams and artistic productions of all cultures in the form of "archetypes" or symbols, such as the witch, the hero, the wise old man. It must be remembered that our species has existed in its *present* form for at least the last 50,000 years. There were, of course, two to four million years of protohuman experience even before this, but the 50,000 B.C. date "fits the sudden efflorescence and diversification of late Paleolithic culture beginning about then." (5) In reference to the Family Unconscious, many of the recurrent patterns we are exploring were established before human beings developed a strong sense of separateness, before the stabilized "mental-egoic" system was instituted, prior to and deeper than our ego-dominated consciousness.

It is important to note in the context of aeons of human history that the collective unconscious is perceived as a region of the psyche in which time is experienced as immanent or eternal, i.e., as timelessness. The personal unconscious, in contrast again to the collective unconscious, structures time in a more ambiguous framework. Time for the personal unconscious can be experienced with a past-present-future dimension. Notice in your dreams how the nonlogical, fluid primary process of the dreamwork can create a situation in which you the dreamer experience an aspect of your past and then immediately project wishes or fears, etc., into the future. A simple example is having a dream in which a childhood bully is scaring you and then turns into your boss who will evaluate you tomorrow.

However, there is also a deep sense or intuition of timelessness in this personal unconscious. This timeless dimension is one reason the unconscious cannot conceive of its own death. We are well aware from Piaget (6, 7) and others that time is a psychological and empirically derived construct and in this sense is extremely malleable. There is the *subjective* "observation" that time, and therefore ultimately space, is also malleable and depends on the observer. We don't have to understand Einstein's relativity to understand this. Therefore we see that, relative to our operating "level" of consciousness, we witness time in a number of dimensions, e.g., one-dimensional (timeless), two-dimensional (past/future), three (past-present-future), or N-dimensional (numerous permutations, e.g., many-worlds interpretation of quantum mechanics). We have our experienced reality in any of those dimensions.

The Family Unconscious, the operational concept we put forth here, is perceived to lie in a sense between the personal and collective regions of the psyche. It shares many of the qualities and dynamics of the personal and collective unconscious and yet is distinct from both. The Family Unconscious is an empirically developed personal system built up through experience but also has certain aspects which are inherited. It is the interface between the system of the collective unconscious with its primordial images and energies and the individualized avenues of the personal unconscious. It is composed of those personal motifs that have been repressed and also cultural and family-interactional styles that existed in some manifestation before the psyche's entrance into that system. In this context the experience of time is again ambiguous for the Family Unconscious.

The Family Unconscious is composed of extremely powerful affective (emotional) energies deriving from the earliest life of the individual. In many ways the Family Unconscious is structured by the recurrent transactional patterns, habitual modes of relating not only by the individual but also by other members of his or her significant family constellation. We draw here from H. S. Sullivan's concept of the dynamism, (8) the relatively "enduring energy patterns" and transformations that occur within the life of the individual resulting from recurrent interaction with significant others. These will naturally include not only anxiety but our early parenting patterns, roles, and styles of interaction that, while once conscious, may be driven to the unconscious dimension of our functioning. Again these include sensory and motoric experiences.

What is most distinctive about the Family Unconscious as opposed to the personal and collective unconscious is that the Family Unconscious contains *shared* images, experiences, and roles held in common by the members of our family matrix. It constitutes a shared emotional field and matrix of consciousness. These shared images and affects are *active, intense,* and *immediate.* They include projective role assignments, collective assumptions, and other functions of the family. (9) At this level of family consciousness, intensity, energy, and affect are shared despite whatever distortions there may be in communication. The effects and affects of this level can be seen in the behavior, roles, and dreams we create. Our examples at the beginning of this book are extreme episodes of this. The reader is asked to note his or her own family gatherings and relations and see how shared assumptions and intense affects are easily aroused and manifested, either positively or negatively but usually mixed, in the family constellation.

A common clinical example is the recurrence of certain psychosomatic illnesses or chemical dependency problems from generation to generation which occurs through the *structuring of intimate relationships* understood as the multigenerational transmission of symptomatology. (10) This involves the passage of symptoms from one generation to the next. It appears commonly in situations where struggles with parental figures over an issue that remains unresolved surface again in the new nuclear family when the child becomes a parent. The child in the later family has focused in on the latent unconscious conflict of the parent and reproduced it, taking a role opposite that of the parent. Also, this parent may be influencing the child, through what is called the projective defense mechanism, to relive his or her own unresolved conflict. The "time" and structure of the original event has remanifested itself in the next generation. The emotional fields of family members become engaged in powerful yet subtle ways. These fields are "between" but also "within" family members and connect but also internally reflect the individuals, both coordinating and enfolding them.

The concept of fields of force or interactional levels borrowed from physics is helpful in understanding this family matrix. *A classical field in physics is a kind of "tension" or "stress" which can exist in empty space in the absence of matter.* It reveals itself by producing forces which act on any material objects that happen to lie in the space occupied by the field. Thus fields can account for action at a distance through empty space and explain how distant objects can act on one another.

The standard examples of classical fields are the electric and ·magnetic fields, which push and pull electrically charged objects and magnetized objects respectively. Faraday discovered that these two fields also exert effects on each other. He found that a changing magnetic field produces electric forces, and this finding led to the development of the practical electric generator. Later the exact laws of the behavior of electric and magnetic fields were formulated mathematically by Maxwell. He found that in any space where a changing magnetic field exists, an electric field must also exist, and vice versa. Later these fields were detected not only in copper wire but in the open air, thus leading to radio and television and their permutations. (11)

Note that space between objects is emphasized. Fields bring objects separated by space into relationship with one another. Even Relativity theory has this "between" notion embedded in it via the idea of signals. In our concept of the Family Unconscious the fields are located not only between individuals but also within individuals. This field is in a sense more nonlocal. Also in this model, traveling through the field are not only the forces known to physics but psychic "energies"—feelings, thoughts, images. Thus we need to distinguish between the classical notion of fields and the newer quantum field. In classical field theory objects are acted upon and respond in predictable, precisely measurable ways such as in gravitational effects on bodies in space or the previously mentioned electromagnetic fields. In quantum fields objects fluctuate constantly and do not preserve a precise position for specific lengths of time. In this quantum field, fluctuations are not precisely predictable, and we are left with only statistical probabilities of fluctuations in behavior averaged over time. We will "flesh" this out as we go along and attempt to further clarify it in the final portions of the book. For now, examples and related models will help to develop the idea by stages.

Now in many ways this shared identity and energy field of the Family Unconscious can be seen as a sub-idea field for all family members to draw from and contribute to. (12) There are numerous and recurrent transactional patterns in which each level of the individual psyche participates. There are therefore in many ways various *levels of awareness* in our individual psychic energy field that interface and interact with other individual psychic fields within our family matrix. This will become clearer as we go along. In later chapters we will explore the family structuring of relationships. This will include the specific developmental tasks of families at certain stages of family growth (13); the family as an affectively powerful psychosexual unit (14); and the family as a dynamic clinical organization. (15)

Of great importance is the fact that the Family Unconscious is to a large extent developed *before* the individual is even a breathing part of the family. We as
individuals are born into a system with a significant part of
the interactions already operative within the nexus. This is
even stronger when there are already many siblings. These
relations or energy patterns can exist overtly within the
family's awareness but are generally unconscious in the
family system. Patterns are established before a baby is born
when there is a lot of discussion about choice of names,
associations of these names to others, cultural demands,
expectations of the new person by the family, etc. In a
sense these roles and energy patterns are implicit, part of
an implicate order of the system. What can be seen as the
shared family superego or conscience and ego-ideal can be
thought of as arising from a sub-idea field and energy level.
The affective energy of these significant others forms a
system that we inherit. Then through our own unfolding
we each make subtle changes in the pattern.

This level of unconscious functioning also continues to
exist after we are no longer an active member of the system.
We note here the family mythology of persons who have
died or left but whose images and example continue to influence others in the system who know of them. A positive
literary example of this is the mode and character of Kunta
Kinta in Alex Haley's *Roots* (16), a saga of an American
family. A negative clinical example is the retained image of
a father or other "bad seed" who perhaps left the family
through a jail sentence or other misfortune. The adolescent
son acts upon the "negative image" others in the system
have of that father or bad seed, leading him to acting out
some of his father's behavior. Needless to say, the clinician
can observe the family's subtle reinforcement of this. Indeed, we all help shape and reinforce each other's unconscious behavior all the time. This of course does not
account for all of the adolescent's behavior, but it points out
one of the profound, covert influences.

2

Related Phenomena

*... mind is unlike the rest of matter in having character-
istics which are apparently trans-spatial and trans-
temporal.*   *J. Hasted,* The Metal-Benders

Often rather uncanny similarities occur among siblings who
are in totally different environments, separated for years,
perhaps not even aware of each other's existence. They
have been found to have not only similar interests and life
styles but also similar voice tone, medical symptoms, and
menstrual symptoms. These similarities were observed in
studies of twins raised apart from each other with little or
no verbal or formal contact between them. (1, 2) Though
raised and named by different parent figures, some were
found to have been given very similar names. Many have
the same personal mannerisms, and some even chose the
same pets. Other studies of separated family members have
also uncovered such uncanny coincidences. (3, 4)

Another interesting phenomenon is that women who begin
to live together in a community or family slowly coordinate
their menstrual cycles. (5) This may be due to the effect of
smell and breath on the human psyche, both individually
and collectively, as will be seen in Section III. Clearly the
coordination or *synchrony* of the group is deeply affected.

These examples lead to the observation that in family-related situations in which people share affect and imagery there occurs a coordinating tendency not accounted for by presently known forces. Heredity obviously plays a role, particularly in the twin studies phenomena, but obviously cannot account for all the similarities.

In terms of the subtlety and range of the Family Unconscious functioning, it is interesting to note that in studies of clinical death experiences persons who have been revived by medical procedures very often report experiences of the observing ego in which other family members, often deceased, are seen. (6) The nature of these thoughts, perceptions, contents, or fantasies, is *irrelevant* here. What is essential is that some form of personal experience, some form of consciousness, continues to exist at least briefly after clinical death. (7) This observed fact may be due to the mass dying of brain cells, or we might speculate that we are born into families, die, and are born into them again. We do not know.° What we do see, however, is that on one "end" of the spectrum of consciousness we enter and on the other end we leave, but the broad region of our shared collective consciousness remains. Before and after each person's life, it remains as an energy field and level of consciousness that we enter, function through, change, and then leave.

Extending this a little further, we note that society, science and culture continue to be unclear as to the beginning and end of life. This uncertainty is expressed though the ambiguity and ambivalence concerning national and state laws and personal beliefs about when the fetus is to be considered a human being. Laws on abortion amplify this ambiguity. As of this writing there is no consensus as to when consciousness and its more intense manifestation

---

°Many cultural traditions around the world attempt to help the dying or dead person move from one "level" to another and may reflect a subtle collective knowledge of this process, e.g. the art of Pho-wa in the *Tibetan Book of the Dead*, certain corrupted Voodoo practices, and other religious prayers for the dead.

termed *awareness* become active in the fetus. Also, on the other end, the moment of death is unclear. Is it when our heart ceases beating for a period of time or when our brain waves stop? With each advance in medical technology this issue will be reopened.

Many reading this are in personal touch with this issue. This ambiguity is parallel to the ambiguity of the exact moment when a psyche's consciousness-force is felt to enter and leave the system of the Family Unconscious. (8) Yogis have shown that a developed consciousness can act as a force which can affect the body, as can hypnosis and bio-feedback. (See Chapter 5.) This searchlights our deepest intuitions of space, time, matter, and energy.

To the objection that the system of consciousness and energy we are outlining is dependent on a nonmaterial substrate, we point out that even those materialists who insist on a "chance and randomness" universe agree in general that the origin of life on this particular planet probably began with certain climatic conditions, bio-carbons, and energy inputs such as lightning. (This makes the creative principle a little like the work of Dr. Franken-stein!) This theory of the origin of life in biochemical terms by Oparin (9) acknowledges that the more highly organized life forms, e.g., warmblooded animals, primates, etc., have complex nervous organizations involving electrical energy and chemical systems that could create or be involved in subtle energy-information cycles and transfers. (10) This implies that there might be different levels of energy organ-ization in the solid, liquid, gaseous, and other states of matter, e.g., plasma. For example, we know that water can be ice, moisture, rain, steam, etc., depending on its energy level. It begs the question of whether such an order also exists in consciousness.

This system or field of the Family Unconscious bears a certain relationship to the influence of morphogenetic fields as hypothesized by Sheldrake. (11) The concept is an organic one taken from the field of embryology. Through these morphogenetic fields information about past experience in a species is communicated over space and time by a process called formative causation. The operation of formative causation is one of the four causal aspects of matter and energy as long ago outlined by Aristotle. The material and efficient causes are well known to mechanistic science; teleological causes have been banished to theology and metaphysics. All four aspects are needed for a full empirical science.

The effects of morphogenetic fields can be readily observed in crystal development and embryology and according to this theory are responsible for the ordering of physical and information changes in a system. These fields cannot be observed directly, as the electromagnetic and gravitational fields are not directly perceptible to the senses but rather are detected by their effects.

The transmission process for Sheldrake is by way of the analogy of morphic resonance, as when you hit the note C on the piano and octaves above and below it respond. While Sheldrake sees no actual energy transfer from system to system, we do see transfer of psychic energy and information exchange in the functioning of the Family Unconscious. As mentioned, mental and emotional energies can be "carried" by this field.

Examples suggesting formative causation and information exchange have been seen in a number of experiments. William McDougall, "far-out" psychology professor, in a series of experiments at Harvard in the 1920's attempted to prove the Lamarckian inheritance thesis but failed by reason of his experimental design and because he did not produce significant differences between his treatment groups (12). In studying the proverbial white laboratory rats' learning ability, he failed because *both* experimental and control groups improved in performance. His results were quite suggestive because each generation of rats seemed to learn the target behavior faster than earlier generations.

Later others took up these suggestive results in their experiments, in this case on the other side of the Atlantic and years later, but found that their laboratory rats started learning at the rate that McDougall's rats had achieved by earlier experience. (13) This appeared nonsensical to researchers, and so still others took up the experiment and found similar results (14). A form of information had been communicated within species across space and time. A similar development of field-information transfer has been observed in crystallized structures with the spontaneous appearance of new forms that are similar to forms observed at other locations on the planet (15). In physics this is similar to the paradox of causality at a distance, or non-locality. We will have more to say of this in future chapters.

Another instance of information transfer within species over space and time is seen in research with monkeys. Here Lyall Watson, a biologist, describes what occurred in a monkey tribe on the northern Japanese islands of the Takasakiyama group. The monkeys refused to eat a new food, freshly dug sweet potatoes covered with sand and grit. They were used to eating foods that required no preparation and were reluctant to eat dirty potatoes.

> Then an 18-month-old female, a sort of monkey genius called Imo, solved the problem by carrying the potatoes down to a stream and washing them before feeding. In monkey terms this is a cultural revolution comparable almost to the invention of the wheel. It involves abstraction, the identification of concept, and deliberate manipulation of several parameters in the environment. Imo taught the new behavior to her mother and to her playmates, who also taught it to their mothers. Eventually all the juvenile monkeys were washing their potatoes, but the only mature adults to do so were those taught directly by their children. Then, quite suddenly, the behavior tended to become universal.
>
> Let us say, for argument's sake, that the number (of potato washers) was 99 and that at 11 o'clock on a Tuesday morning one further convert was added to the fold in the usual way. But the addition of the hundredth monkey apparently carried the number across some sort of threshold, pushing it through a kind of critical mass, because by that

evening almost everyone in the colony was doing it. Not only that, but the habit seems to have jumped natural barriers and to have appeared spontaneously, like glycerine crystals in sealed laboratory jars, in colonies on other islands and on the mainland in a troop at Takasakiyama.

Watson commented:

> The relevance of this anecdote is that it suggests there may be mechanisms in evolution other than those governed by ordinary natural selection. I feel that there is such a thing as the Hundredth Monkey Phenomenon and that it might account for the way in which many themes, ideas and fashions spread throughout our culture. (16)

We have observed similar ideational and affective phenomena within family constellations.

Finally, the reader is directed to the observations of experimental physicist John Hasted who has observed repeatedly that some subjects who watch certain psychic episodes in person or on television often are able to perform the same action. (17) He observed and tested adults and their children who could bend metal without touching it, through psychokinesis. The process occurs very often in the family constellation, and he notes repeatedly the influence of field and unconscious influences. He terms this learning over a field *induction*. In each of the above examples of related phenomena the reader has been able to see influences between intimate relationships that are mediated by unconscious forces or interactions most often occurring in a family constellation.

In essence, then, we have come to see the Family Unconscious evolving in the following way: It appears to be a level of consciousness that lies in the region of the psyche "below" the personal unconscious and "above" the collective unconscious. Its powerful affective energies are the result of recurrent transactional patterns with our significant others over time. These recurrent transactional patterns are largely inherited through our established family patterns and are also added to by the psyche's empirical work and experience. This region of shared imagery, expectations, and affective energies generates and participates in a shared idea-field that influences the individual psyche at great and short distances. This influence is prior to us and persists after us. We influence this system while we are members of it and as such contribute to its evolution.

The Freudian unconscious is characterized by energized emotional complexes of an intrapsychic nature. These are established by empirical development. The Jungian collective unconscious is characterized by universal archetypes shared by humanity from time immemorial. The Family Unconscious is characterized by present *shared affect* and *imagery* of the family's psychodynamics. Its reach touches both empirical and universal or inherited dynamisms, and yet is exhausted by neither.

Clinically speaking, a dynamic manifestation of the operation of this Family Unconscious can be seen in family therapy sessions. Here we can witness the various levels and subtleties of relationship, particularly in the exchange of symptoms and the dreamwork of different members. Every family therapist has witnessed the exchange of symptomatic behavior between family members over the history of the problem, and what physician has not noticed the uncanny similarity at times of spouses' illnesses? We all shape and reinforce each other continually, consciously and unconsciously. In sharing the dreamwork during sessions, the therapist can see the various projections and distortions in addition to the strengths and supports of the family system. Dreams of each member will reflect his or her particular skew or view of the shared family affective matrix. The holographic model, in which information about the whole is encoded in every part, is helpful here. For a therapist working in such a system, it is crucial not only to be in touch with, but to trust and actively use his or her creative unconscious, along with other methodologies, as an avenue of insight in restructuring various impaired transactions or ways of relating.

It is not too much to point out that this shared affect-idea field of energized relationships is constantly operative. Families may persist for centuries and leave indelible influences on a city or culture, e.g., the de Medici family of Michaelangelo's Florence, or the Bach family in Baroque music. Or they may endure for only decades. Their influence, both subtle and philosophical or grand and political, however, may persist for even longer periods of time, though in much less intense form. In both an individual and collective sense, we all create and participate in those deep family images and patterns that, borrowing yogic terminology, we might call "family samskaras."

It is a datum of modern science that energy can never be destroyed, only transformed and/or transmitted. Though it has never been measured directly and is known only indirectly by its effects in hypnosis and biofeedback, there is growing evidence that "thought" is a form of energy. If thought is not completely dependent on space and time, then on some level and in some permutation of the original "thought germ," all the thoughts and ideas that ever existed exist now in some form. The collective unconscious is conceived as an organized psychic energy level of these thoughts, thoughts that have their more affectively intense or vital manifestation in the personal and Family Unconscious. The Akashic records (18, 19) of the yoga seers, and the *Alayavijnana* or store consciousness of the Mahayana Buddhist school (20) refer to these still vibrant thought-energy forms which we think of today as part of the collective unconscious.

In a very real sense, this storehouse of the Family Unconscious and its wider interface with the collective unconscious influence is prior to and "deeper" than our own individualized or "mental-egoic" experience. When we lose intimate connection with some kind of energy of the Family Unconscious and fall prey to the illusion of absolute autonomy or individuality, we run the risk of real illness and a loss of the sense of being grounded. Dynamic interconnectedness or interdependence is vital to our well-being.

Each reader either struggles or has struggled with this issue of autonomy and dependency, be it during adolescence or earlier. Embedded in it are our ways of handling loyalty, commitment, personality, and psychic boundaries, and the host of other family-related issues. These we will return to in the final chapter.

However, even deeper than this is information about ourselves that unites us with all other families and perhaps all other beings. If one had the correct way of decoding or transforming this deepest energy level (the correct Fourier transform), one would have access to this vast field of information. On principle, we believe this is possible.

SUMMARY

We have come to see the Family Unconscious in ourselves and others as a dynamic stratum of *shared* imagery, idea, and affect that operates in the life of the individual and in his or her family context. This system exists prior to the individual and is altered in its evolution by the individual. It is composed of the recurrent transactional patterns of the person and the systems in which the individual participates through his or her relationships with significant others. This level of consciousness has information structured within it and to a large extent exercises a formative causal influence on individual behavior and psychodynamics. This operates across both space and time. It has certain similarities to other processes in nature.

We shift focus now to that realm in which space and time are not only repeatedly demonstrated to be flexible, but which erupts into and canvasses our affective and psychodynamic life. This is our nightly inner landscape we call the dream. We plunge now into that matrix, that intimate shared field of the family unit, as it unfolds around and within us.

II
Family Dreams

Like unto the ocean-waves
Which by a raging storm maddened
Against the rugged precipice strike
Without interruption;
Even so in the Alaya-sea
Stirred by the objectivity-wind
All kinds of mentation-waves
Arise a-dancing, a-rolling.
                    Lankavatara Sutra

3

The Dreaming Night and the Clinical Office

The family molds the kinds of persons it needs in order to carry out its functions, and in the process each member reconciles his past conditioning with present role expectations . . . . In the struggle, the choice of particular defenses against anxiety is also selectively influenced by the family pattern.
Ackerman, The Psychodynamics of Family Life

THE INNER LANDSCAPE

When Yoda, the Jedi master of the *Star Wars* series, was training Luke Skywalker in the ways of the Force, the young initiate asked him where the Force came from. Yoda looked around him at the trees, the stones, the vast contours of the planet itself, and said it came from everything, that all life generated it, that it could be felt between the water and the air and even between the leaves themselves. Luke could not see it and walked away. Then Yoda demonstrated the subtle/immense power of the Force by bringing up Luke's sunken spaceship from the planet's muddy swamp and presenting it to him. Luke watched in astonishment, repeating, "I can't believe it." Yoda then said, "That is why you fail."

This chapter is certainly no revelation of the Jedi. Our aim is much simpler. Yet we will deal with an experience as universal and omnipresent as the Force—our dream life. If we look closely, we will see our dreams, like the life force the Jedi saw as interconnecting us all, influence not only ourselves but those around us with whom we have intimate contact. Here we will demonstrate how the Family Unconscious operates through dynamic affect and symbolism within the context of the individual psyche and the family matrix. Clinical examples taken from case histories will be presented in order to flesh out the schema we advanced in the previous chapters. As you read through these examples, please reflect on your own dream life and, if possible, on the dreams of those very close to you in an intimate and/or family setting, so that you can examine the process yourself. We focus on the dream life of the individual and the family, using a model of consciousness based on field theory, to amplify the shared idea-affect nature of the common field that is both between and within individuals. For the time being, we will stay within a psychodynamic context.

For years folk wisdom, clinical evidence, and theory from a wide spectrum of research and experience has indicated that parents, parental figures, and significant others mold, expand and in innumerable ways differentiate the personality of the growing child. (1, 2, 3) These significant others affect the emotional and also the cognitive life of the developing person. (4) Freud (5) in his early psychoanalytic explorations was not the first to realize this, but he was the first to chart this inner landscape in a coherent, operational way. This led to the recognition of repression as an active psychic force to the major defense mechanisms, and of course to the vast ocean of unconscious psychic energy patterns, identifications, and transformations. The processes of the dreamwork such as condensation, projection, and symbolization are well known. Who of us has not seen several events and people actually separated by years combined together in our dreams, placed in a somewhat new yet strangely familiar setting, doing some occasionally unusual and/or emotionally powerful action? Space, time, and events are easily recombined in our inner landscape of dreams.

The dominant culture in which we live has an immense impact on how we respond to our dream life. Depending on the relative value our culture places on dreams and dreamlife, we come to recognize their influence in our waking life or vice versa, and we either attend to dreams or reject them as totally meaningless, thus repressing or ignoring them. Dream interpretation is hardly new, and its systematic application is clearly an ancient, and often intuitive, art. There are the dream interpretations of Joseph in the Bible, and those of the Greek poet Simonides, to mention only a few. These were rooted in the cultural-symbolic interpretation of mind and nature for Western man in that age. With the arrival of Freud, Adler, and Jung, the role of observation and consensual validation was introduced such that others could also understand the once largely intuitive process. At present, as we enter more deeply an age of systems thinking and holistic interpretation of experience, a different scheme of dream interpretation is emerging.

We assert here that dreams provide a meaningful source of material suitable for an understanding, not only of our intrapsychic life, but also our interpersonal, family-intimate, and greater collective psychic experience. As such, dreams can be extremely useful as an adjunct to many forms of psychotherapy and as a mode of communication drawing friends and intimates closer together. The claims for the use of dreams in therapy itself are not new by any means. What we find of particular value here is the use of dreams in a family and family therapy context with a dynamic systems and shared consciousness model.

The use of dreams as a reflection of each level in the personal system, i.e., the intrapsychic, interpersonal, and then family-intimate and collective system, has certain advantages and disadvantages. The obvious advantage in a family therapy context is that the significant others of one's life are present. That dream discussion can be a way of re-opening blocked family communication is already established. (6) In the family therapy context, however, there is the possibility of emotional catharsis and potentially the restructuring of family relationships using material elicited in the dreamwork.

The disadvantages have more to do with the specific

theoretical interpretation by competing schools of thought over the *content* of dreams. The approach advanced here focuses on the *process* itself, the forms and styles of relating, rather than the content or specific meaning of the dream-work. The intense emotional situations of family members are expressed in the dreams of each member.

THE ENFOLDING NETWORK

The following dream recurred often to a fifteen-year-old girl who was in treatment along with her family. She dreamed that she "escaped" from her parents' house and jumped into their car. As she drove away, the father ran toward her but never managed to catch her. The closer he got, the faster the car went. Finally she fully escaped from him—only to run headlong into a telephone pole and suffer instant death.

In this family's therapy sessions, the themes of autonomy and separation with accompanying anxiety erupted repeatedly. This oldest child also fought with her parents over her intense involvement with a young man. The girl felt dominated by and rebellious against her parents, in particular her father. However, when she stayed away from home too long she began to experience somatic complications and wanted to "lose herself" in other males.

Another dream by this girl's twelve-year-old sister revealed a similar theme. The younger sibling dreamed that a large "awful man" ran around screaming at her mother, her older sister, and herself. Finally the man stepped on all three but did not kill them. This dream also recurred several times with slight variations. The family that provided this dream series was composed of a father who had a manic-depressive disorder, an extremely religious, compulsive, mother, one female adolescent, and another pre-adolescent sibling. The two girls dressed as if they were in their mid-twenties, and were somewhat stylized and pseudosophisticated in appearance. All three females had somatic complications, i.e., stomach cramps, persistent gas pains, migraine headaches, and frequent depressive episodes. The father did not want to present his own dreams.

From the girls' dreams it can be seen how a particular significant event or constellation in the family may be viewed by each member in a particular way, and therefore how the network of family relationships is contained in each of these events. The holonomic model of everything reflected in each individual is helpful here, and in later chapters we will explore it in greater detail. Each family member, through a succession of such events in the family life, takes his or her own identity from this network. (7) Because each "significant other" is present in the therapeutic situation it is possible to explore and clarify these levels and modes of communication, to make *explicit* the "role projections" and distortions in the family, and to realign these disordered relationships. (8) In the case of a healthy family system, such exploration can increase true empathy and acceptance of differences, thus avoiding unresolvable conflicts.

The dreams of any "significant other" in the family reflect his or her particular skew or perception of that family's constellation and conflicts. The unconscious understanding and assumptions about how the family network operates is expressed in the dynamic structure of the dreamwork. The *process* rather than the particular *content* is the focus. The therapist begins to see that each family member is in touch, often intimate touch, with the significant other's undercurrent of feeling, though she or he may not recognize the particular situation depicted in the dream. When there is an interface between these affect-idea fields in the family, it is often the most painful or the warmest aspect of the relationship that finds submerged expression in the dream. The same dynamic situation is often seen in the group process. (9)

Work with patients and their families leads to an uncovering of these relationships of whatever content and often reveals long suppressed rage at infantile losses. We are here concerned with those patterns that operate in the present life situation of the patient. Strong, unresolved dependency needs and associated anger are clearly observed in parent-child relationships.

Take the following sequence from out-patient family therapy. Mrs. P., the mother of the fourteen-year-old male identified patient Steve P., was confronted in several family sessions by her six children who claimed she was overprotective of them. Whenever any of them became involved in disputes at school or home, Mrs. P would become very agitated and proceed to scapegoat Steve, the middle child. When the siblings, half of whom were adolescents, were not engaged in some kind of dispute, she would complain that they were just waiting for a good opportunity to do so. In this way, she covertly reinforced an expectancy of such behavior in the system and also attempted to bound her own anxiety by keeping a tight rein on her children. Several times during family upheavals she had a variation of the following dream: "There is a storm and I'm out by myself... (people) don't even speak to me ... I'm trying to get home on dark, windy streets." This reveals her fear of isolation, of being abandoned, which she projected into waking life using those around her to avoid this catastrophic situation.

Remember that the *Alayavijnana* or store-consciousness of the last chapter has "thought-germs" that are projected outwards in the system. The same mother had another dream in which she reacts to the potential separation from one of her children. She dreamed that "I let N. go with a strange man and a girlfriend of hers and a little boy. They went to school somewhere up the turnpike. I had a disagreement with the other mother to follow and catch them." The ambivalence over separation is here reflected in the psychological split of the mother and "other mother." In family therapy, this "stranger" was associated with her husband, the father of the family. Both members of the marital pair admitted the distance between them had grown since the six children were born, and that they would have some adjusting to do after the siblings left home. The subtle power shift and fear of change in the marital relationship employing the siblings and especially the scapegoated child is manifest here. Mrs. P. was generally an agitated and depressed woman during sessions. A common theme in all her dreams was traveling, a metaphor useful in dream series. The possibility that one of the marital pair had begun to consider separation could not be ruled out. Neither, however, admitted to such thoughts or fantasies.

The dreams of families in and out of therapy reflect the major emotional issues of that family. In addition to the in-dependence-dependence struggle of autonomy mentioned earlier, there are powerful recurrent issues that arise around specific stages or crucial periods in family develop-ment. (10) The initial stage of parenting and the dynamics of the family romance can be seen in all stages, but appear particularly intense in the early stages of family life. The adolescent years bring on the issues of separation from the family of origin and generate somewhat different dynamics. Mrs. P. had difficulty when her children began to reach this stage in the family cycle.

As the family becomes more differentiated, the new role expectations, distortions, family alliances, and sibling con-stellations emerge, finding expression in each family member's dreamscape. The holographic model is useful here since each position in the hologram has embedded within it the perspective of each other position.

One pre-adolescent male, S. W., not a patient and also not from a family in treatment, had the following recurrent dream concerning his newly arrived younger male sibling: "I dreamed that M. turned into a large bird in his crib. When he would do this, he would then fly away." This is a common sibling rivalry dream. What made it difficult for S. W. was that the child died suddenly (crib death), and he was overcome with guilt and grief. His mother dreamed that her own mother, now deceased, had come and taken the dead child away, ostensibly to help him. The mother experienced guilt also, but none of these feelings were directly expressed until years later. The archaic reasoning of the sibling seems to have been tapped by the mother.

The family experienced a normal extensive grief-work period.

Family alliances are most clearly reflected in dreams when there is intense marital discord and the products of such conflicts we often see as the "identified patients" in the family system. An adolescent, who was an inpatient, repeatedly dreamed that mother and father were leaving the house but stopped at the door, or else they returned to the house when the adolescent, as a child in the dream, began to cry or scream. As long as the child cried, the parents were together with him. When the crying stopped, the parents prepared to leave. The process of the dream reflects not only the identified patient's dilemma, but also the triangulated structure of the family's marital relationship.

Thus in each tissue of dreams occurring in the family system, the fields between individuals and within individuals can be seen to interface, and information is shared with varying degrees of clarity. This draws us toward specific ways to explore this process.

4

Family Dreamwork

Perhaps we may call the dream a facade, but we must remember that the fronts of most houses by no means trick or deceive us, but, on the contrary, follow the plan of the building and often betray its inner arrangement . . . . We say that the dream has a false front only because we fail to see into it. We would do better to say that we are dealing with something like a text that is unintelligible not because it has a facade, but simply because we cannot read it.

C. Jung, Modern Man in Search of a Soul

Readers may want to use some of the following methods for examining and working with their own and their own family's dreams. Most of what follows can be used by clinicians, but it is by no means confined to the treatment setting. Dream understanding is no more the exclusive provenance of the therapist than crop production is that of the professional farmer. What issues from the local garden is just as nourishing in most cases.

The suggestion that the family in therapy keep a dream log is often initially resisted by the family. Its members naturally want to know what relevance this has to the presenting problem. By briefly demonstrating or explaining the technique as a way to better understand each other's feelings, the therapist can begin to gather more clinical data. The ease or difficulty with which this suggestion is taken can indicate to a considerable degree several dimensions of the family's operations. It indicates the family's style or response to intrusion, its boundaries, its degree of engagement or disengagement, and clearly its projected image of itself to outsiders. Who responds first? Who is the family hero? Which ones are emotionally allied? What is the "atmosphere" of the problem presentation?

In working with family systems, we have noticed consistently the sharing of spontaneous early family fantasies once the process has been accepted. These family fantasies are rich in mutually shared family myths, e.g., the "fragile one," the "crazy mother," etc., and have embedded in them the implicit roles and identities the family has developed to cope with its own exigencies and stresses in the wider community. The Family Unconscious begins to emerge as this dream log procedure is used, a procedure that again can be easily demonstrated for the family. (1) The "homework" required to tabulate dreams is minimal since only a few dreams are needed to provide rich clinical data. In terms of the pathologically enmeshed family, dream reporting and work lead to more differentiation of family members, since the subtleties and figures of personality emerge more clearly against the background of shared identities or fusion relationships.

Several methodologies are applicable in this functionally oriented approach. In working with such families we have found some techniques to be more productive than others in eliciting and working with the dreams of a family member.

A *contrast* approach can be used by comparing and having each family member compare the different interpretations of one member's dream in the family session. Generally in the early sessions this member is not the "identified patient" so that the role of the "patient" is not reinforced for him or her in the therapy group. In time, the identified patient's dream is focused on, and by then the therapist may have clinical data to reflect to the family that the "sick role" in the family is not fixed on one person, that it travels at times from person to person, and perhaps that eventually the role is not even necessary.

This contrast technique can be further explored by having various members free associate to the dreamwork.

The similarity of associations used by different family members will lead the therapist to observe several other dimensions of family functioning.

The therapist will notice to what extent the family system is one of fusions or enmeshment. (2) The interface of family systems of identification and communication becomes more elaborated. An overinvolved or highly enmeshed family is one in which the social roles are static and closely knit. Children cannot leave home even for awhile without their feeling guilty and the mother becoming depressed and upset. Communication is often not a "communicative intimacy" (3) but one in which orders or expectancies are carried out. In the family characterized by pseudomutual relations, there are rigid adaptations to external realities and no internal warmth prevails. People are understood almost completely in one role such as "father" with no variation allowed. The schizophrenic adaptation may take root here. In both family styles, the shared dreamwork can be quite emotionally evocative and as such must be executed with skill and compassion.

The family system in which fusion occurs is one in which the associations of one member are very similar thematically to those of another. In one family, the daughter in a triangular relationship had associations to the dream that were extremely similar to the mother's. The daughter was the mother's rival to the father. The direction of the therapy session was toward a clearer overt realization of the identification of the daughter with the mother. At that point it was easier to lead into work on the competition between the two and the reciprocal way the father infantilized both and reinforced their dependency needs. The intense similarity between dreamwork associations of two or more members of the family begs the question of an even deeper communication between family members that *employs* the language and medium of dream symbolism and meaning.

Another technique is for family members to simply say what the dream means to them, calling particular attention to the fact that they are not saying what it means for the dreamer but rather how the dream reflects on themselves.

This avoids overanalysis of the dream. It also provides an opportunity for each member of the family to speak and be reinforced for such expressive and exploratory behavior. In a highly fused family it also offers an approach to differentiating members from the family unit by way of reinforcing each member's exploration of his or her own individual system of ideas, associations, and affects.

A third and similar technique involves having each family member tell a dream in the first person even when he or she is not the dreamer, and then working with the meaning and significance to each. This again gives the family and the therapist a workable view of the family communication process. It provides working data for a therapeutic restructuring of family relationships.

In all the techniques mentioned above, it is extremely helpful and at times crucial that the therapists have available to them their own personal and shared Family Unconscious. Indeed, the trust in the therapist's own unconscious is in itself a certain methodology for dealing with the fluid dynamics of primary process, nonlogical, emotional events in the core of a family affective field. This "creative unconscious" can manifest in numerous ways.

There are other elaborations and techniques that a therapist and family may use with this model of family process. What is central is the perception of the family as an organic whole with mutually interlacing modes and levels of communication. The dream is the more primary process mode and closer to the heartbeat of the family.

SUMMARY

It has been the observation of clinicians and family therapists that a family's recurrent transactional patterns are reflected in their dream life and that these dreams, when reported and worked with, provide useful material for the family therapist and the family seeking a greater understanding of itself. The dreams and dynamics of family life reflect a host of dysfunctional patterns, e.g., double-bind situations, projected role distortions, and traditional attempts at conflict resolution. In the presence of the significant others in one's life these irrational role assignments, distorted communication patterns, and dysfunctional attempts at problem solving can be restructured and given a new direction. The reflection of the family's process through reflection of the shared dream's process opens the way to overcoming denial, scapegoating, and other resistances. In nonpathologically oriented families, which include the vast majority of families, the process can reflect healthy coping mechanisms and aspirations and serve to deepen the sense of family intimacy. A lower incidence of "mental illness" is found in families that observe this process and in cultures where dreams are normally shared. (4)

The operation of these family dynamics through dreamwork sharing reflects the various interactional patterns, family styles, and energy relationships that influence the personalities of family members. This level of shared imagery, idea, and affect again comprises the Family Unconscious. It is likened to a hologram in which each section of the hologram has implicated within it each other section or reference point.

It has also been our repeated observation that there is a high number of uncanny similarities in associations to dreams by different family members. We have gained the impression that these dreams and energy dynamics are sometimes employed to communicate even deeper levels of information between intimate people, levels that do not appear to use the usual sensory channels. What is the source, the origin or focus of this information that emerges in the family and individual context? Clearly, while it may not be confined to biological and sensory processes, it must be related to our organism and organization. It doesn't just come out of the blue. Before we explore more deeply the operation of these modes of information sharing, we must examine their source. It is to this radiant focus that we now attend.

III
The Radiant Organism

It is possible that there exist human emanations which are still unknown to us. Do you remember how electrical currents and "unseen waves" were laughed at? The knowledge about man is still in its infancy.

A. Einstein

5

Energy Systems of the Body, Yoga, and Biofeedback

There are places in your body you have never been.
F. Will Our Thousand-Year-Old Bodies

The great extension of our experience in recent years has brought to light the insufficiency of our simple mechanical conceptions and, as a consequence, has shaken the foundation on which the customary interpretation of observation was based.
N. Bohr, Atomic Physics and the
Description of Nature

In a passage from one of his many provocative explorations, Werner Heisenberg, one of the fathers of modern physics, stated that in the history of human thinking some of the most fruitful developments frequently take place at those points where two different lines of thought meet. While working in the area of family systems and also in the use of biofeedback treatment, I have observed a number of interesting developments. This section will present some of those lines of development for both theoretical and practical purposes. It will be helpful, therefore, to divide it into two general sections. The first chapter will present theoretical and research findings related to these developments, providing a few clinical examples as done in earlier chapters. Secondly, we'll look at and experience these phenomena that we present in such a way that you may directly experience them yourself. In both instances they will reflect on the operation of the Family Unconscious in the family matrix or field and in the individual person of the family system.

Now, exactly what are these energies that function as a field within us and between us and our intimate, significant others? From where do they arise? How are they sustained and propagated? Do they just appear out of nothing, random and inexplicable like waves in a storm at sea? We have advanced the idea in Chapter One and Chapter Two that the Family Unconscious operates as a field of influence in the family that affects our dreamlife, our cognitive development, and exists as a system prior to and after our functioning through it. It is a form or permutation of energy that involves mentation and psychic forces. This is across the usual boundaries of space and time.

The human body, its nervous system, and the *organization* of the physical-psychic system is seen to be the individual source of these manifesting energies. Our organism remembers, perceives, and responds not only with conscious memory, but also on motoric and sensory levels. After you burn your hand on a hot stove you don't have to debate this issue again; your body responds immediately in future situations. We register events constantly and continually respond with the organism on multiple levels. These levels include our autonomic nervous system, the various levels of the unconscious, and the many shifting energy levels of the body. We know from psychosomatic illness that mind can influence the body negatively at a motoric and biochemical level. We know mind can also influence and change the body at subtle levels through techniques such as passive attention in biofeedback and hypnosis.

There is no reason in principle to limit the reach of consciousness to these. Indeed, we have only to peruse the extensive clinical and experimental literature in biofeedback alone to see how the focusing of attention and consciousness toward specific areas in the organism can bring out radical physical and psychological changes. It seems as though our intentionality reaches subtly into deeper and deeper regions of the body and material world when we cultivate such skills. These radical and also subtle alterations include selective amplification of the autonomic nervous system (1), EEG brainwave functioning (2), cardiac activity (3), blood pressure (4), and a legion of other clinical areas.

It has been demonstrated that a relatively normal person from the general population can be taught to control specific muscle components or individual motor units in the body and even create rhythms in single muscle units with practice. (5) In fact, a number of investigators have even demonstrated that it is possible for a client to affect a *specific* nerve cell with his or her consciousness. (6, 7) Since this can be done with relatively little training in terms of years, it is certainly feasible to see how a trained and sustained consciousness can be directed to affect progressively more subtle aspects of the physical body. There are numerous experiments conducted in the U.S.S.R. that demonstrate an individual's capacity to influence blood-sugar levels by thought alone. (8)

These more subtle aspects and techniques all serve to "quiet the vital," that is, the powerful somatic and emotional energies, and increase conscious control. Perhaps as one "deepens" his or her influences of consciousness on and in the body, he or she begins to contact that level which appears "inanimate," such as oxygen and iron molecules which enter from the environment. Clearly with greater subtlety and control, gross distinctions between animate life and the inanimate molecules in the body become blurred.

This whole area of clinical research has initiated a profound revolution in the West on how consciousness can regulate the neurophysiological level of our being. The physical energy and consciousness levels appear to us totally coextensive. For example, I vividly remember a session with my massage therapist Kathleen McG. in Northampton one Friday when very early memories of childhood were awakened. These were similar to experiences I had much earlier when a Rolfing specialist gave a demonstration to our clinical group at the hospital where I completed my post-doctoral training. Years later, using the EMG (electromyogram) in our biofeedback clinic with focused concentration, I was able to experience again these tangible yet primary process mental energies. I saw for myself how various physical techniques can affect consciousness.

A good deal of excellent research after deep muscle massage or structural integration termed Rolfing has replicated that an energy field, measurable by instrumentation, can be observed not only around the whole body but actually concentrated in specific areas. (9) These areas are associated with the endocrine system and involve subtle biochemical processes in the body that have to do with cellular activity in regions associated with freeing "blocked" energy. We will look at this more closely in the next chapter. Suffice it to say here that these areas involve intense affect or emotional/psychic energy and can be directly influenced by consciousness. You can observe this in yourself by remembering what happens in your shoulders or stomach when you get angry.

The whole area of psychological stress and its effect on the body has reached the general public by T.V. and magazine. This includes subtle brain chemistry, e.g. endorphins and neurotransmitters, and probably certain cancer processes (e.g., T-lymphocyte and macrophage inhibition). Thus the psychological-affective field we posit in the individual profoundly influences our subtle physiological and cellular-endocrine system. It is only a matter of time before we realize the influence of consciousness on the chemical, then atomic, then subatomic or quantum level. Of extraordinary importance is the simple fact that we respond not only to our own consciousness, but that we respond to the affectively charged consciousness of those significant others in our life who are part of our Family Unconscious.

A number of other experimentally oriented researchers working in the area of biology and physics have presented data that appears to substantiate the active existence of a biological energy field within living organisms. Drs. Harold S. Burr and F. S. Northrop in the 1940s at Yale University advanced their Electrodynamic Theory of Life. (10) Using sensitive voltmeters they measured voltage gradients between different areas of the human body. The gradients were simply differences of electrical DC potential and must not be confused with the electrical currents found in the brain or skin. When the instruments are sensitive enough, the field can be detected even without skin contact. Burr and his coworkers found a characteristic field, what they termed "L" or Life field, in every kind of living form they examined. In addition to this, they found the L field was constant in its rhythmic pattern even after the molecules of an organism had been completely replaced by other molecules. Increased DC electromagnetic flow was associated with feelings of well-being. The body was seen to have a number of subfields of energy that interact with each other. Burr stated repeatedly that these were true energy fields and not skin resistance or G.S.R., as some suggested. These fields were seen to be intimately connected to the *organization* of life. Sometimes there were observed changes in these L fields preceding physical occurrences and symptoms, including ovulation and malignancies.

In terms of biofeedback, we have seen a number of clients who, after some instruction and information about psychophysiology and concentration, are able to alter these energy fields for clinical gain. Mrs. R., an attractive, perceptive 50-year-old woman, had suffered from mixed migraine and muscle contraction (tension) headaches for more than a decade. She had consulted various headache clinics and was compelled to use increasingly powerful medication to control the pain. She also experienced mild Raynaud's disease, a vascular problem resulting in cold hands and feet much of the year. After only four sessions, she learned to eliminate the symptoms. We used a combination of sustained diaphragmatic breathing and mental focus on the sensation of warmth in her hands and coolness, when appropriate, in her face. Internal imagery, focusing on the exhalation phase of the breath, led to positive results. Follow-up several months later revealed no return of symptomatology and no use of medication. She was required to practice daily for ten minutes and at the onset of any sense of a headache. A similar sequence of events was observed with A. Y., a married woman with headaches during stressful periods usually involving her family of origin. In this situation, some brief psychotherapy was required in addition to biofeedback as described.

We have also successfully treated irritable bowel syndrome, hypertension, chronic pain syndrome, and to some extent pediatric migraines. However, not all cases are successful and resistance emerges here as it does elsewhere in psychotherapy. Occasionally, a client has exchanged one syndrome for another.

The use of subtle consciousness in a "passive-volitional" mental framework was effective in altering various somatic and energy fields in the body. In this regard, we mention that to increase warmth in specific areas of the body by thought and imagery is to effect thermal energy flows of the system. To change EEG patterns is to influence the electromagnetic field of the brain. These are only two examples. The immune system itself is influenced by emotional and psychological factors and has a memory for earlier disease processes, and thus it is in some sense intelligent. This perhaps helps explain why such subtle levels of the body are open to psychic influence by way of sustained imagery, affect, and passive attention. We have found it extremely useful clinically for the therapist to feel coordinated in-breathing and motivation with the client during treatment.

These fields can be understood in standard electromagnetic terms and quantitatively measured. A similar phenomenon is seen in acupuncture, used therapeutically for ages in the East. That does not necessarily mean that acupuncture lines or meridians are pathways of electromagnetic energies. Indeed, the acupuncture theory identifies the *Ki* or *Ch'i* force of acupuncture with other energies. (11) Almost every human culture has made a similar observation and labeled this force or energy. (12) The Hebrews called it *Ruach*, the Congolese *Elima*. The Algonquin Indians named it *Manitu* and the Sufi *Baraka*.

The Burr work on L fields and the more simple biofeedback cases are empirical support for these organized fields and relationships in and around the body. Notice that Burr detected the field at some distance from the body.

Research in the Soviet Union has also focused on this area. The general term used is *bioplasma*. Here it is noted that the spine appears to be the center of bioplasmic activity (13) which is also stressed in yogic literature, where the spinal energy system is termed the *Sushumna*. Several replicated findings appear to characterize the bioplasmic field of the body as including ions, free electrons, and free protons. (14) This field is highly conductive and provides opportunities for the accumulation and transfer of energy within the organism as well as among different organisms. Bioplasma is considered a fifth state of matter as explored and developed by a rigorous technology. To be more specific, it has been noted by Inyushin and others that bioplasma or biological plasma exhibits:

> the presence of delocalized electrons in the form of pi electrons; the existence of semiconductor properties in cell membranes; high concentration of unpaired electrons in biologically important molecules such as DNA and RNA; the presence of electrical polarities in organisms; the semiconductor properties of chlorophyll and the independence of the photosynthesis process on temperature; the collective character of the changes in the density of quantum processes under the effect of physical factors, as when mitogenic radiation is created in visual fields when light hits the retina of the eye; and the creation of electrical fields by frictional changes concentrated on the surface of the body, fields that can be detected at distances away from the body. (15)

Inyushin hypothesizes that the organism's bioplasma is an important factor in bioluminescence, which is the emission of photons or light particles from organisms such as fireflies from causes other than high temperatures.

Thus several lines of research, some modern (Burr, Inyushin, and others) and some ancient (acupuncture and the subtle body of yogic science), point to the existence of an energy field or energy body manifesting in and detected at some distance from the organism.

This energy field has a dynamic behavior that does not conform to our presently established laws of biology and physics. It has thus also been given the name *biogravitational field*. This biogravitational field is intimately connected with our recurrent emotional and cognitive life, and thus is intimately involved with the field of the Family Unconscious. For that reason we quote Dubrov at some length as he details the biological and physical workings of this field:

> From certain data it can be inferred that a biogravitational field arises in an organism in consequence of changes in the conformation of protein structures as a result of the transformations which occur with polypeptide molecules. This is the body of bioplasma with its abundant ions, free electrons and free protons spoken of earlier. These changes in conformation include a strictly ordered, structured crystalline state in the hydrated protein molecules and their *oscillations are synchronized*, as a result of which a qualitatively new physical situation is established, effecting the atom's symmetry groups and the nature of the *sub-molecular space* . . . a variable biogravitational field . . . is contingent on the phased oscillations or rotations of hydrogen electrons or atoms in water molecules. (16)

The mechanism outlined above is operative since in each cell of our bodies, including your body and my body at this very moment, the protein molecules together with the layer of intracellular water adjacent to them are in coherent, high-frequency oscillatory states. (17) In other words, the protein and water molecules in our bodies vibrate synchronously. We are vibratory creatures. It should be remembered that our human organism is largely composed of water, i.e., hydrogen and oxygen, in a highly complex organization.

This biogravitational field has very little "power" as calculated by Dubrov, Bunin and others (they place it at

10^{-23}W). The issue, however, may not be the power of the force, but its sensitivity, range, and selectivity (see Appendix A). This biogravitational field of the organism as outlined by Dubrov has certain properties in common with natural "forces" in nature: a) it acts at close and long range as does gravity; b) it can be detected and *focused*; c) it can be positive or negative and thus cause attraction or repulsion; d) *it can carry information*; e) it is able to convert the energy of a field into matter with weight, as in psychokinesis; f) a field of such force can *persist* in the absence of the source which originally gave rise to it; g) it is closely bound up with changes of symmetry groups and with the distortion of space at the submolecular level of biological structure. There is reason to believe that consciousness pervades even unto the quantum level.

Dubrov has shown how these synchronous vibrations (waves) or levels lead to the increased generation of biogravitation of the bioplasmic field in the form of an "energy body." This energy body is totally co-extensive with our denser material body, and the two influence and exchange with each other, as would be expected from Relativity theory. We see that this energy body can be detected and unconsciously directed and altered.

When these phased oscillations become more synchronous and the organism moves from a less well-organized state to a more ordered state, the "density" of the biogravitational field increases. This exerts a greater influence on other biogravitational units and the fields of other individuals with whom one is in harmony or phase coherence. We may surmise that this harmony or phase is provided by shared imagery, affect, and recurrent transactional energy patterns. This in turn can be seen as a shared field of energy relations that comprise the Family Unconscious. Each psyche in the matrix is in some degree of phased coherence relationship or resonance with all the others on multiple levels. This is especially true in the exchange of what we conceive to be affective energy. There is a constant energy manifestation through what can be termed biogravitational waves from each organism. Organisms affect each other via these waves at close and far distances.

In the dreamlife of the family the operation of the Family Unconscious is seen as we have demonstrated in clinical detail in Chapter 3. What we observe here is that each unit in the family system is constantly radiating various energies into the greater field around it. These energies are electromagnetic and also biogravitational, and they involve thoughts and feelings. Both issue from the energy body of each individual and expand or radiate in certain "frequencies." This may occur, not only in a linear or spatial way, but also in some other "order" or level. These frequencies are capable of information transfer at significant distances from the generating unit.

Actually as we think about the energy field of the organism we come to realize that the material "stuff" of the body is constantly being changed through time while the field remains intact. All the molecules in our bodies are completely replaced every five to seven years. If we slow down our perception, as occurs in some forms of meditation, we can come to actually perceive a quiet exchange with the environment by way of breath, discarded cells, etc.

When is the inanimate oxygen and iron from the environment involved enough in my bloodstream to become an integral part of my waking consciousness? My "boundary" is open and tenuous, more a function of my level of observation and time perception than an inherent separation from the surround in time and space. Our energy field is always, on some level, transcending or oblating the usual waking experience of time, i.e., our identity persists through space and time. We refer back to the open "ends" of the shared consciousness continuum of the Family Unconscious where the issues of the beginning and termination of life and consciousness for the organism are blurred. The energy field extends beyond the solid body's fixed position in linear space and time and yet interfaces with it at innumerable levels of interaction.

6

Autonomic Nervous System
and the Science of Breath

*We are confronted with an entirely new conceptualiza-
tion of our inner being which is radically different
than our traditional notions of body-as-machine. The
quantum theory overturned Newton's clockwork,
deterministic universe and its billiard-ball-like elements, and erected in its place a cosmos with different
complexions of space, time, mass and causation. If
quantum physics wrought such a revolution in our concept of the nature of the entire physical universe, we
can expect it to wreak astonishing transformations in
our views of our psychophysical self, an expression of
that very universe.*

L. Dossey, Space, Time and Medicine

The dogwood bloomed in the sunlight of spring my third
year of graduate school. I was having a fervent love affair.
Our relationship was intense, recurrent, and meaningful to
me. We had to part when the school year was over. Three
days after she left town, I sat in the apartment with my
graduate student roommate, Jake Lessewing. It was a warm
afternoon. Suddenly a little after 2:00 I felt an intense pressure in my chest. I "knew" that the woman I was involved
with was in trouble. The experience came as a vague sense
emotionally, but physically it was quite distinct. It was
similar to an anxiety attack, though we were relaxed and
there was little academic pressure now. It was nearly two
weeks later before I received a letter from her stating that

53

at that very time she had been involved in a minor auto accident that required brief hospitalization.

My body, on a subtle level, had somehow registered this event, even though my cognitive framework only dimly recognized the situation. The reader may have had a similar experience, either through a conscious experience like the above, through a dream, or by some other pathway. This chapter will look at the physiological level of this process, a process that was communicated by the energy system of the body-mind field that interfaces with the Family Unconscious.

The previous chapter focused on the source and generation of this energy field in its various forms, from biofeedback to L fields to the Russian research. We saw how to some degree this field might interface with the shared imagery and affect of the Family Unconscious. This energy body has various names, both ancient and modern. The science of yoga recognizes several interpenetrating fields at different levels within each of us. The *pranamaya kosha* or subtle body is the field of vital energy and is intimately connected with the breath. This section will focus briefly on this energy body so that you may directly experience at least part of it yourself.

Many psychotherapies such as the Bioenergetics of Alfred Lowen already use the energy body concept when working with intense affects and blockages of energy in the body. (1) Wilhelm Reich, for another example, explored the manifestation of subtle energies in the body via its expression in a person's "character armor." (2) This is the habitual muscular, visceral, and breathing tension postures which are somatic expressions of psychological defense mechanisms and personality styles. While these energies may differ somewhat from the biogravitational field, there is little doubt that with some practice one can personally experience these aspects of the energy body and know their functioning.

The electromagnetic fields of Burr and the energy body of Lowen strike us as connected instead with the "denser" organization of matter and more directly under the manipulation of the ego. Their manifestation through body posture and the breath are more overt than this and as such closer to direct intervention by the therapist. This level corresponds to the yogic *pranamaya kosha* associated with vitality and breath. Biogravitational fields, however, appear to involve information transfer at a distance and require more mental or subtle energies. These latter actions and energies are usually acknowledged to occur when there is a suspension in the realm of the ego, as we shall see in the next few chapters. In yogic literature, this mental sheath or field is termed the *manomaya kosha*.

Medical science has repeatedly shown how the mind affects the body. It is not at all unusual for a client in a clinical hypnotic trance to use deep, internal imagery to cause a change in a specific region of the body. The use of biofeedback in behavioral medicine attests to the focus of consciousness interacting profoundly and intimately with the physical level. One way that body/mind interaction is mediated is through the breath.

The breath can be both voluntary and involuntary, and the "energy body" of the organism can be directly influenced by it. The reader's experience is invoked here. By executing a simple breathing exercise you can go beyond suggestion to the direct experience of the energy body. Using the technique of slow diaphragmatic breathing and alternate nostril breathing as outlined below, you can begin to mildly experience the energy body in a relaxed, expansive subjective state.

The technique is termed *nadi shodhanam*. Before starting, structure the situation so that you will not be disturbed by others and there will be a minimum of environmental distractions. Then place yourself in a comfortable posture, preferably with the spine straight from base to crown. The spine has a gentle curvature which should be supported at the base. Your body should be still. Bring your right hand to your nose with your index and middle fingers held down in such a way that the right thumb is used to close the right nostril and the ring finger is used to close the left nostril. With the right nostril closed by your right thumb, *exhale* completely through the left nostril. It is important that your exhalation be *smooth, slow,* and *deep.* At the end of the exhalation phase, inhale slowly through the left nostril and fill the lungs. After full inhalation, close the left nostril with the ring finger and exhale through the right nostril. After full exhalation, inhale through the right nostril and again close the right nostril, exhaling through the left nostril. Remember to breathe slowly, evenly, and diaphragmatically. The duration of inhalation and exhalation must be equal, and there should be no sense of exertion. (After practice over time, the duration of inhalation and exhalation can be gradually increased.)

Continue to focus your attention only on the sound of the breath and either in the center of your chest or slightly above your eyebrows in the middle of the forehead. Repeat this pattern three more times for a full cycle of five complete breaths. When you have completed five full cycles, rest your attention at the root of your nose and breathe slowly. Your subjective state will be obviously altered. You will see that breathing and consciousness are interrelated. If your biogravitational or energy field were measured before and after this exercise, definite differences would be found. Perhaps you caught a sense of this subtle field as you did the exercise. The accomplished yogi can slow his or her respiration to seventy-six cycles per hour through what is called *Ujjayi pranayama* and thereby deeply influence the subtle energy body.

The olfactory nerve responsible for the sense of smell is linked to the limbic system that is the biological substratum of our emotionality. It is a curious fact that this nerve has a 1½- to 2½-hour cycle of either left or right nostril dominance. In other words, we breathe primarily through the left nostril for 1½ hours or so, and then primarily through the right. (3) Neurophysiologists and rhinologists have found that inhaling either clean air or air containing substances that can be detected through smell stimulates the olfactory nerve, which can affect emotion. This natural alternation of breath from nostril to nostril has been intimately associated with laterality of brain functioning discovered by ancient yogis, and it appears to affect the functioning of left- or right-hemispheric modalities. (4, 5)

Much of this can be understood as the ability of the breathing techniques described above to increase awareness and control of the autonomic or involuntary nervous system. The autonomic nervous system is divided into two areas, the sympathetic and the parasympathetic. The sympathetic nervous system governs the more active, externally oriented functions of the system. When the sympathetic system is activated, the heart rate increases, adrenaline is secreted and a host of other responses occur, signaling intensified arousal, commonly called stress. The parasympathetic system governs more resting functions such as digestion, relaxation, etc. An optimal balance between the two is essential to health. Excessive sympathetic activity is associated with hypertension, cardiac problems, tension and migraine headaches, and other stress-related problems that have been treated in biofeedback. Excessive parasympathetic activity is associated with depression and certain vegetative disturbances. Each inhalation stimulates the sympathetic system; each exhalation stimulates the parasympathetic system.

By slowly learning to regulate the motion of the lungs through the observation and control of the breath, you can also regulate the heart function by way of the vagus nerve. Then the right vagus nerve is slowly brought under conscious control and that portion of the mind-brain interaction that coordinates the involuntary or autonomic nervous system is brought under control. There is also a direct line to the internal organs of the body through the vagus nerve. (See diagram.) Thus many functions of the autonomic nervous system can be controlled. This system is intimately related to the conscious control of the breath.

It is clear that with effort and practice, the involuntary systems become progressively more open to conscious

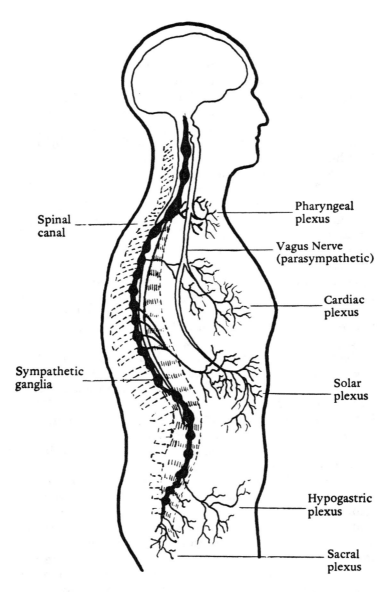

Spinal canal

Pharyngeal plexus

Vagus Nerve (parasympathetic)

Cardiac plexus

Sympathetic ganglia

Solar plexus

Hypogastric plexus

Sacral plexus

Autonomic Nervous System and Plexuses

Reprinted, by permission, from *Science of Breath* by Swami Rama, Rudolph Ballentine, M.D., and Alan Hymes, M.D. ©1979 by the Himalayan Institute.

voluntary influence. "All of the body is in the mind, but not all of the mind is in the body" is how Swami Rama explained his remarkable abilities at the Menninger Clinic. He produced at will various brain wave patterns, stopped his cardiac functions, and created a difference of 10° F in two areas of his hand at the same time. (6) This was done by the science of breath control or *pranayama*. According to yoga philosophy the energy system of the body is a subsystem of the energy system of the mind.

The yogic breathing techniques of pranayama are a direct way to influence the nearly 6,000 miles of nervous system within the adult human body. Through practice the 500 cc we regularly breathe is greatly expanded in the full diaphramic breath to 3000 cc. Think of it as our primary energy exchange with the environment. You and I can survive perhaps a month or more without food. We can go almost a week without water. How many minutes do we have without oxygen?

Recent data on the physiological changes in the organism using the breath and certain yoga techniques and postures demonstrate the operation of the energy field. (7) These include the above-mentioned autonomic functions (cardiac and respiratory rates, blood flow, endocrine and brainwave alterations, etc.), all of which are intimately associated with various states of consciousness. In other words, a certain state of consciousness associated with breathing techniques can subtly influence these areas of the body-mind field. Simple diaphragmatic breathing and alternate nostril usage will induce a state of autonomic balance accompanied by calm and expansiveness along with the capacity to slow down the rate of thoughts. Reflection solely on the breath flowing evenly at the root of the nose and relaxation of the body will lead to a pleasantly altered state of perception and experience. This is an early phase of many types of meditation, and it also marks the dawn of direct knowledge of one level of our radiating, information-processing energy body.

We have seen that this energy body is a vibratory body

that interfaces our mental-affective field and also the physical body. As such, it is in intimate contact with that greater resonating field of the Family Unconscious on many levels of interaction and influence.

SUMMARY

These chapters presented the Family Unconscious as a level of energy and shared consciousness that has as its generating source our biological organism and organization. The field was used to demonstrate the integration of these levels of consciousness *between* and *within* organisms and organizations. We also identified for the reader a direct experience of this energy body.

We also differentiated between levels in this energy system, i.e., the "denser" field of the energy body and the "finer" field of the mental realm. Both are deeply affected by and can be consciously influenced by the breath. The conscious experience of these more subtle energies will reveal the formative or organizational influences of these fields, leading eventually to their control. And yet even without conscious control we see evidence of their perpetual operation in our everyday life. It is to these more subtle energies, these presently obscure aspects of consciousness mediated by the shared Family Unconscious, that we now turn.

IV

Psi, Dreams, and the Family Unconscious

The image of self and image of family are reciprocally interdependent.
  Ackerman, The Psychodynamics of Family Life

The entire difficulty with the psychologists, then, boils down to something that can be settled by experiment. Better still, the experimentation has already been done. The answer to the representative psychologist's rejection of ESP because it doesn't make sense in physical terms is that it is now experimental fact anyhow. The metaphysical assumption is itself in error. The assumptions of science have to give way in the face of contradicting facts, or science would not fit the realities of nature.
  J. B. Rhine, New World of the Mind

In the Eastern view then, as in the view of modern physics, everything in the universe is connected to everything else and no part of it is fundamental.
  Capra, The Tao of Physics

7

The Sinew of Consciousness

I dreamed my genesis in sweat of sleep, breaking
Through the rotating shell, strong
As motor muscle on the drill, driving
Through vision and the girdered nerve.
                    D. Thomas, Collected Poems

Who of us has not personally experienced or does not know a friend or family member who has not experienced something similar to the following account:

In the dream, I was walking along the street. No one was around, but at a distance I saw a black-draped figure approaching whom I finally recognized as a favorite aunt of mine. She had on long flowing black robes and a black hat with a brim and the hat had a heavy black veil over it which covered her face.

I laughed when I saw her because she is such a neat, well-dressed person that I couldn't imagine her being dressed in such unbecoming attire. I remember I continued to laugh as she came nearer and nearer. I could see her face; and she didn't smile. She just looked at me and then passed me without saying a word. This too was shocking because she and I were *quite close, more like mother and daughter.* Then, as she passed, in reality someone began knocking on the door. I answered, and it was my landlady telling me someone wanted me on the telephone. It was this same aunt calling to tell me my grandmother (her mother) had passed away. (1)

This event involved death. Many involve potential danger to a family member and loved one.

In some accounts there is actual verbal/mental communication between family members involved in the crisis situation:

> My son had been home on furlough from Mississippi, and I had taken him to the depot late at night to take a train back to camp. He asked me to go home and get some sleep. He didn't mind waiting alone.
>
> Two nights later I was sound asleep when I thought I heard a loud knock on the kitchen door. I got up and turned on the kitchen light, then opened the door. There stood my son. He had bandages on his legs and tears in his eyes. I said, "Come on in."
>
> "I got lost from the other boys tonight," he said. "I was in a swamp. I just wanted to come home and see you once more. Now I have to go back and see if I can find them."
>
> He turned and went down the steps toward the garage. It was raining a little—foggy—he just disappeared in the fog. I shut the door—and woke up.
>
> I stood there frozen in my tracks. I knew it was a warning or a vision. I went back to bed after praying for my son's safety.
>
> Two days later I received a letter from him. He said, "The first night after I got back we went on night maneuvers. I was sent back to camp for something we forgot. I took a shortcut and got lost. I was really lost for hours. I didn't think I would ever get to see you again. I prayed I would find my way out of there. But I followed a light, like a star, and finally came back on the road."
>
> Was this a dream I had, or a vision, and did my prayers help him? (2)

Experiences like these are common to our species and have been an aspect of our shared life and shared consciousness long before the dominance of language. Stimulus-response psychology is vacuous in the face of such experiences. Even the intrapsychic model is overly strained in attempting to account for these events. What is required to make some sense of these phenomena are models of interconnectedness, shared inner landscape, and dynamic affective influences. For this we draw from the Family Unconscious concept as previously elaborated.

While paradigms do not die gracefully, they often yield to sudden or gradually overwhelming data that lead to their being supplanted by systems of knowledge that incorporate them. This is the situation with the science and methodology that has developed around the phenomenon of psi experience. Psi has often been an umbrella term that included various areas of experience and research, e.g., psychokinesis, precognition, clairvoyance, telepathy, and other domains. This section will limit itself to the body of experimental and clinical literature that relates to the phenomenon of telepathy. Telepathy is conceptualized as the awareness of information exchanged between persons without use of the traditional sensory channels. The above cases are examples from real life, not the laboratory.

In this chapter we will present the history of psi research with examples of particular problems and the modes of psi exchange. The next chapter will include the operation of the Family Unconscious and the dream life of persons as a medium of psi interaction. The third chapter will focus on the sensory exigencies of psi behavior, including sleep and other forms of external sensory withdrawal. The fourth chapter will focus on the process of the psyche's "focus and field" behavior and its involvement in the psi transmission. The fifth and sixth chapters will make explicit the various channels of affective-imagery "exchange" that characterize the shared energy-consciousness field of the Family Unconscious. The final chapter will present some detailed clinical observation of this process in the clinical hour and in the home setting. Subheadings will group material so that you can easily follow the presentation and examples provided. You may wish to note any similarities to your own personal experiences in the examples given.

HISTORY, METHODOLOGY, AND SCIENCE

Ever since the groundbreaking work of J. B. Rhine (3, 4) and associates in the early and middle part of this century using an experimental and statistical methodology, there has been a steadily accumulating pool of data from this traditional model of research that suggests there are "holes" in our concepts of what constitutes physical and psychological reality. Rhine not only catalogued and replicated over and over many diverse psi phenomena using a rigorous methodology, but his wife and coresearcher Louisa also catalogued and outlined an impressive array of "subjective" forms of spontaneous psi experiences more difficult to replicate. (5) Later in this chapter numerous incidents and experiments of the psi process will be presented. The problem has now become, not whether psi exists, but in what ways psi manifests itself, and what its implications are for our lives, particularly for those who work in the field of family and group systems analysis.

In 1973 a survey of the scientific community taken by the *New Scientist* (6) revealed that 67 percent of responding readers (mostly scientists) concede ESP to be an established fact or likely possibility, and 88 percent thought the investigations to be legitimate. One early review of modern scientific paradigms by the Stanford Research Institute offered the conclusion that "these [psi] phenomena are not at all inconsistent with the framework of modern physics: the often held view that observations of this type are *a priori* incompatible with known laws is erroneous in that such a concept is based on the naive realism prevalent before the development of quantum theory." (7)

There is clearly a growing shift in the scientific perspective on psi phenomena. With an increasing understanding of various levels and forms of energy relationships, we are being drawn toward a major reevaluation of the place of consciousness in our world view. What was for nearly a century considered epiphenomenon or merely a passing shadow of our neural latticework is now being recognized as an intimate aspect of reality.

This plunges us deeply into the scheme of the scientific method itself. John Wheeler, a leading theoretical physicist, extends the earlier developed implications of Heisenberg's principle of indeterminacy (1963). He points out that because of the very nature of consciousness, the observer's involvement in an experiment is a determining factor in the outcome of that experiment. He suggests substituting the term *participant* for *observer* to remind us of how central and active the effect of consciousness can be. For modern physicists consciousness has become a fact and force greater than that which is attributed to it by most psychologists. Even psychologists who accept the concept of "participant observer" are usually operating from an earlier, more traditional mechanistic-energy paradigm. In the light of the revolutionary view of consciousness by some physicists and the self-regulation of neurophysiology through biofeedback and yoga, the older model is beginning to spawn numerous anomalies.

It seems natural that psychologists and others working intimately with families and interactions between psyches pay more attention to these developments. The mechanistic and organic models of psychology have greatly advanced our science of mental life. However, we are also beginning to witness data that do not fit neatly into these models. In the areas of systems thinking, dreamwork, and family therapy, it appears that a "field of relationships" is available to account for much of the above-mentioned material. The implications are enormous. But just what types of data and exactly what situations lead to a reevaluation of the older perspective? In order to approach an operational answer to this, we need to utilize a number of models or schemas. Each has a unique feature that offers certain helpful ways of organizing data. However, the territory is not the map.

One of the early areas of new data issuing from experimental psi research was the relationship between personality and psi experiences. Schmeidler and McConnell (8) summarized material on personality and psi and also experimentally confirmed numerous times the so-called "sheep-goat" pattern. This pattern demonstrates that subjects who tend to believe in psi, termed "sheep," consistently and significantly score higher in standard ESP guessing experiments. Those termed "goats" were inclined not to accept the psi hypothesis and also scored lower. When this and related phenomena were repeatedly confirmed by others (9, 10), it became clear that the disposition and emotional feeling or attitude of the psyche deeply affected the intimate operation of this process. The degree of "openness" of the personality system to such phenomena affected its operation and reception. Here we literally can see and to some extent measure the direct effect of consciousness in an experimental situation.

There are a number of different trends in scoring that repeat themselves in psi testing. These have been given many interpretations, but they are not all understood at present. (11) Personal motivation has a profound effect in the psi process, and this has led to research which confirms repeated patterns of interaction. The importance of the experimenter or observer on the whole process has become apparent. (12, 13, 14) The emotional and psychological relationship between persons in an experimental situation reveals a field of interaction that requires that experimenters and therapists continually assess their own effect. Furthermore, there is no traditional stationary or "objective" position from which to observe. Ego or "I" and non-ego interact in ways in which the "boundaries" are not always firm and impermeable.

The boundaries and emotional relationships between subjects have been tested using physiological methods. Dean (15) designed an ESP experiment with 20 cards. The first five cards contained names chosen randomly from a telephone book; the second consisted of friends of the experimenter; the third contained names of people with whom the subject had close emotional ties. The last cards were control cards and had no names. The subject was attached to the plethysmograph which measures the volume of blood in a finger. This gives an indication of emotional or autonomic system arousal. The recording mechanism was placed in another room with the experimenter and an observer. The experimenter shuffled the deck, chose the top card, concentrated on the name, and attempted to communicate extrasensorily with the subject. Dean found statistically significant data confirming that the baseline of the plethysmograph of the subject fluctuated more markedly while the experimenter focused on the names of people with whom the subject had a strong emotional relationship. This suggested that the subject responded neurophysiologically to communication between himself and the experimenter, and that this communication was registered by the autonomic nervous system.

Tart (16) replicated and extended this finding. He attached percipients (receivers) to a plethysmograph and to an electrocardiogram (EKG), which monitors the electrical activity of the heart. The agent (sender), situated in another room, was administered mild electric shocks. The receiver was not informed of the purpose of the experiment. Still the receiver demonstrated sudden alterations in their neurophysiological signs when these shocks were administered to agents. Again the autonomic nervous system appears to be involved in this information and energy transfer from a distance.

In the area of psychodynamics Freud, along with another psychoanalyst, Wilhelm Stekel (17) noted that telepathy occurred often in dream states. He felt that we would more likely observe such communication if we took cognizance of psychodynamic mechanisms. Burlingham (18) noted a high incidence of psi communication in analytic observations of children with their mothers. Ehrenwald (19) has increased the number of such psi observations between mother and child. This situation involves the archetypal event of nurturance and will be elaborated later.

One of the persistent findings that goes against our centuries-old working paradigm is that space and time do not operate in a sequential-linear way in the psi process. In other words, the three-dimensional space-time framework of Euclidian geometry breaks down in these regions. We have intellectually known from Einstein's work that this indeed is the case as Einstein demonstrated the relationship of space and time and energy in a non-linear model of reality. However, this had not become part of our intimate reality until psi experimentation created a body of research which reinforced the innumerable spontaneous cases. Great spaces do not appear to prevent the operation of psi.

We are also aware that the psi experience can be differentiated from other experiences, that is, has certain recognizable features that you and I can detect under the right conditions. (20) In the majority of studies concerning this, a state of deep physiological relaxation was employed, or what has been termed in other research as a state of cholinergia. (21) The state of cholinergia involves an activation of the parasympathetic division of the autonomic nervous system. The opposite or sender state is termed adrenergia. The state of adrenergia is the intense activation of the sympathetic division of the autonomic nervous system. In the cholinergia state the person/psyche becomes relaxed, open, expansive. In the state of adrenergia the psyche is intensely focused, alert.

Cholinergia as a state of mind receptive to psi has been studied extensively. Hypnosis has been employed experimentally to create and deepen this state. (22, 23, 24) The dream process in combination with hypnosis dramatically increased psi success. However, just relaxation without hypnosis or dreamwork also slightly increased the rate of psi recognition. (25)

In all the different types of paranormal experiences, almost all studies report dreams to be involved in 33 to 68 percent of cases. Close blood ties are involved in about 50 percent of these cases. In connection with this intimate reality, Puharich, the researcher who first used the terms *cholinergia* and *adrenergia*, noted that his subjects often seemed to experience a sense of "the centrifugal reach of ... mind in the state described .... It appeared as though ... mind was a collecting vortex for people who had a deep personal meaning." Thus the state of cholinergia and adrenergia appear to be a dynamism of energy exchange and transformation between emotionally connected people. The number of accounts of psi mediated dreams in that other family-like emotional matrix, the psychotherapeutic setting, are extensive. (26, 27)

The death of someone close looms as the most prominent theme, being present in close to 50 percent of these experiences, with accidents and injuries next in order of prominence. This is termed "crisis telepathy." These dreams that are psi mediated are most often experienced as vivid dreams, dreams of a particularly vivid, intense nature which tend to have a "tenacious quality" to them after the dreamer awakens. We will look at this closer in the next chapters.

From only a sketch of the above data taken from a greater body of research literature, we begin to see the following: 1) Psi phenomena do occur in many different contexts and do not appear to be random. 2) Personality and *motivational* factors have a profound effect on the occurrence of psi phenomena, and motivation in part reflects our psychological processes embedded in recurrent transactional patterns. 3) There are definite feelings and subjective states which are associated with these occurrences which appear to be conducive to psi experience. 4) There are definite trends in response patterns to phenomena such as the aforementioned "sheep" and "goat" styles, the famous "decline effects" where high initial interest leads to high positive scores and vice versa, plus other motivational influences that have been repeatedly validated experimentally and 5) space and time are variable phenomena or constructs within our own nonlogical, primary process intrapsychic world which often direct or inform our assumptions and exclude the possibility or perception of other assumptions. In other words, these modes of perceiving determine the way we experience the world and prevent other types of experience.

We are driven to conceptualize the new data emerging before us, not in terms of static space and time categories with their assumptions of energy transfer, but rather in a model of quantum levels of energy with a space-time variability as found in modern physics. (28, 29) Along with variability of space and time, psi is tremendously influenced by affective states and subtle energies and the effect of personality, motivation, and intensity of interpersonal relationships. Because of these factors we are drawn back to the common dreamlife of the individual and family. As we saw in Section Two, perceptions, affects, and symbols are less defended against in the dreamlife and there is a vital network of enduring relationships. It is here that psi makes use of dreams and affects in order to manifest.

8

Dreams, Energy Systems, and Family Life

Sleep navigates the tides of time.
D. Thomas, Collected Poems

In dreams, dwelling as they do in the inner landscape of the unconscious, we are free from space and time constructs of waking life. Symbols, images, and affective charges predominate. Things can become their opposites, and a different language rules. The dreamlife contains and reflects the "field" of our cognitive and emotional life. We saw this explored in earlier chapters. This dreamlife has access to our deepest memories and structures for the recognition of reality. This "field" of energy relations has levels of intensity, patterns of interaction, affective charges to persons and events. It operates prior to and is "deeper" than our conscious equation, including our "mental-egoic" aspect. It is in the context of intimate and family relations that we see these dynamisms operative. The family's influence on character development and cognitive structures is awesome. This occurs whether or not one is fully differentiated from one's family of origin. In respect to psi phenomena, clinical and experimental investigators have noted the unusually large number of telepathic dreams shared by members of the same family. (1, 2)

In our discussion of the Family Unconscious, we stressed Freud's awareness of family influence on both the intra-psychic and dreamlife of the individual. The earliest work by family-oriented therapists elaborated on the influence of family dynamics in the structuring of conscious and un-conscious functioning. (3) Research expanded to include the family as a psychosocial organization. The experience of certain primary images, affects, and themes in action in the family was a notable step forward in our understand-ing. (4) Other studies explored the family as a unit and its implicit and explicit rules and roles that exert a profound effect on the individual's interpersonal and intrapsychic functioning. (5) The subtle influences of the family con-stellation on the source of comfort or disease and illness in the family were studied. In particular, how the influence of family rules and roles affects "unhealthy" behavior was mapped. (6, 7)

The family conveys or transmits styles, including characterological types, attitudes, and personality traits. From these cognitive styles and character types we can see that certain recurrent transactional patterns or ways of re-lating lead to a stabilized energy system and solidify rela-tionships within a family. We carry these "deep structure" patterns outside and beyond the family. It goes without saying that our children pass them on to their children. This occurs regardless of whether these patterns are healthy or not, or even reflect the schizophrenic constella-tion. (8, 9) The unhealthy family can even sustain intense delusions in the face of contrary facts when its shared unconscious is cathected or deeply invested in a theme or themes. (10) There is little doubt today that the family is the bedrock of learning and the deep structuring of rela-tionships. (11) In each phase of family life—from early parenting days to the loosened energies of adolescence on through eventual struggles with autonomy and separation to recapitulation across generations and wave-front inter-actions—there are definite tasks and dynamics. Seeing a developmental pattern with specific tasks at specific stages is helpful here. (12) This interweaving of patterns and energy also helps us come to see how these patterns are not located totally within an individual but *within* and *between* individuals in the overall family system.

A model of consciousness based on field theory satisfies certain "neatness of fit" conditions.

The above perspective relates to psi in the Family Unconscious in these ways: 1) Families use the occurrence or networks of psi much more than people who are unrelated to each other. 2) Families can and do structure roles on a deep intrapsychic as well as interpersonal level. These structures influence the transmission and reception of psi information. 3) Families teach not only overt values but structure cognitive styles and powerful unconscious affects and images. These influences are often beyond the awareness of the waking ego.

Interweaving of patterns and energy among family members helps us to view the individual psyche as an open system, as opposed to primarily intrapsychic models. The possibilities for perceiving how psi events occur become expanded. (13) The waking ego is no longer experienced with rigid boundaries, and yet it remains a stable system. In an open system the control and also, most importantly, the limits of the ego and the exact boundary between the psyche and other psyches becomes more tenuous. In other words, the boundary between ego and non-ego becomes much more open to negotiation. Factors which blur the boundary are *shared* psychological imagery derived in part from family relationships, a mutual behavioral field at times, shifting individual intrapsychic boundaries, and earlier powerful affective relationships. Some have pointed out that psi first manifests itself in the earliest of all human relationships, that between a mother and child. Indeed those first weeks and months are symbiotic of necessity. Others demonstrate and replicate experimentally that psi occurs with some regularity in dream states between persons who know each other (14), while closer emotional ties bring it to even sharper focus. (15)

When we refer here to *the unconscious*, we do not mean a spatial location. The spatial metaphor creates certain boundary problems to the imagery of the unconscious. Rather, we conceptualize conscious and unconscious aspects of the self as different energy levels or frequencies that can coexist in the same space, but at higher or lower levels of vibration. It is like music or resonance, which can be simple, multiple, or complex, with many high and low frequencies, but requiring no more space.

The use of dreams in family therapy has been presented earlier. It should be noted that psi is known to occur in other family-like relationships. In other words, whenever the affect between people is intense, the motivation for communication is high. This means psi will occur not only in very strong family relationships (whether biological or legal-social), but also in those of a psychological nature, such as between a therapist and client. (16, 17)

An extremely interesting finding for many psycho-analytically oriented investigators is that psi dreams often occur for the patient when the patient feels neglected by the analyst. Also they tend to occur when an unresolved problem *on the part of the analyst* is reactivated by the patient's effort to deal with the same issue. We feel that in families, too, the members unconsciously taking in each others' concerns (transference and countertransference) creates a network of affective energy relationship in the family. There have been a few uncompromising observers in the analytic hour who have noted the occurrence of the psi episode when the therapist allows his or her counter-transference or unconscious factor to operate. These observers include Freud, Deutsch, Hollos, Hitschmann, Hann-Kende, and of course Jung. Sometimes the content of these psi events can be daily problems and not necessarily tragic situations. (18) In either case the unconscious dynamics of one psyche are powerfully cathected to or invested in the unconscious dynamics of another along some emotional/psychological matrix of energy that incorporates or touches the "boundaries" of the other.

Interestingly enough, a client's psi experiences are often reported, but rarely those of the therapist. Here is an exception that concerns Freud himself:

> [Freud's] first observation of this type goes back to 1919, when after the Great War Freud was greatly pleased by the visit of Dr. Forsyth, the noted London analyst, to his Vienna house. Freud being engaged with a patient, Dr. Forsyth left his visiting card with the message that he would call again. While dealing with his next patient, Mr. P., Freud was still thinking of his distinguished guest—the first foreigner to visit him following the cessation of hostilities—when this patient unexpectedly produced the name *Herr von Vorsicht*. This is the German equivalent of Mr. Foresight, a name closely resembling that of Dr. Forsyth, and the patient mentioned it with reference to his own story. From the analytical point of view this reference fits in well with the patient's general attitude to the analyst. Freud interpreted it as an expression of his jealousy of the stranger to whom the analyst's attention had been diverted from him. Here again the point is that the patient could by no conceivable "normal" means have learned of the doctor's presence in Vienna and still less of his visit to Professor Freud. (19)

We are compelled to look for the general patterns and conditions of psi experiences that occur spontaneously within a highly charged emotional network such as the family or family-like relationships. Rhine's work indicated that 40% of a person's dream life concerned some family related matter. Often family crises were dreamed about, but significantly, despite the considerable diversity of dreams, only a few *general family themes* emerged. In the chapter on affective currents and levels of consciousness we will see these themes operate.

Note that the following series of dreams involving close relationships occurred in psychological and physiological states conducive to psi retrieval as outlined earlier. Also note that certain psi interchange patterns are witnessed using the dynamism of cholinergia and its opposite "sender" state of adrenergia.

A man working in a city sewer doing repairs becomes trapped by a cave-in. He is alone, frightened. A minor earthquake has caused the cave-in and a painful injury. The excited, frightened man [a state of adrenergia] 'flashes' on a close friend he knows across town. No one else can hear the injured man's call for help. The distant friend is working outside in the street [miles away] in a boring, repetitive job and is lulled into a state of relaxation (state of cholinergia). He has spent hours in the warm sun operating a jackhammer. The injured man continues, in fear and pain, to think of his friend. He thinks of him visually. The friend feels uneasy and makes a rationalization of why he leaves work early and goes to the other side of town to the exact street. The friend eventually checks where the workmen's tools are in the street and soon locates his friend. (20)

Sometimes the members of a family may actually share the same imagery and emotional tonality.

An adolescent wakes suddenly from sleep [i.e., relaxed state of cholinergia] in which she remembers no dream and perceives a distinct image above her in the room. She is sure she is not dreaming. The image frightens her but eventually dissipates. The next morning the adolescent hears her father telling her mother of the same image that appeared to him the night before. The adolescent then confirms her experience with the rest of the family. (21)

Sometimes the family theme and image will repeat itself.

During WWII a man's sister, M., is stationed as a WAVE in Washington, D.C. She becomes ill and is hospitalized. One night M. dreams that she is sitting on a high wall—if she lived, she would have to stay on the wall, if she fell, she would die. Thankfully she lives.

Several weeks later her father contracts pleurisy and is dangerously ill and hospitalized. The family, feeling that M. will worry [collective family thought], and that M. was already so ill, decide not to call her home unless absolutely necessary. One night after a visit to the ill father by the family, the door to the room opened and there was M. demanding "where is Dad and *how* is he?" It seems M. had

had that same dream, but this time their father was on the wall, so she went AWOL and rushed home, knowing instinctively that their father was very ill. (22)

It would appear that psi is more likely to occur in these altered states. To be sure the boundaries of the waking ego are more or less permeable with regard to psi processing when more relaxation is used, but these phenomena are more likely to occur in these other altered states. These altered states include full, deep relaxation, dreaming, hypnosis, sleep and meditation. In fact, research using meditation has indicated that psi phenomena can be more easily recognized and the person's ability to demonstrate the phenomena may also increase with deepening practice. (23) Others have shown and replicated these findings using different types of meditation, which of course lead to different meditational experiences (24). It is most interesting in this regard that much of this research is paralleling what has been known and taught by other scientific and meditational procedures for many years (25). This we will explore in detail in the next section. In each case there is an increase in the activation of the deep relaxation response and other functions under the control of the parasympathetic division of the autonomic nervous system. Sleep is usually a relaxed state, a state where cholinergia predominates. The sudden intrusion of powerful affect and imagery can shift one from one state to the other. The pattern is not linear but multi-leveled and in some as yet unclear way, can be predictive of the future and beyond the constraints of linear time.

It was five years ago; I was eighteen years old. I woke one morning after a restless night with a very vivid dream imprinted on my mind. I often wake remembering my dreams, but this one bothered me particularly. My mother at that time slept on a Hide-a-bed in the living room, I in a bedroom adjoining. My dream started with Mother and me standing in a certain spot in the living room, looking down at the body of one of our best lady friends lying dead on the Hide-a-bed.

Everything was exact. I was standing a certain way, my mother the same. She sobbed five words, 'She was my *best* friend.' The dream ended and I woke up. I simply couldn't get this dream out of my mind, but I shrugged it off more or less because it seemed very unlikely that this friend would be dying anywhere, but particularly unlikely that it would be on *our* Hide-a-bed. She was in perfect health at that time and still is today.

Exactly one month from the day of the dream it happened, but the situation was reversed. My mother died in her sleep of a heart attack. I awoke to hear her gasping, called the doctor and this friend immediately. The doctor arrived first and pronounced my mother dead. My friend came in, and we both assumed the exact positions as in my dream and she said the very words in the same tone of voice. (26)

Here is another example that defies linear time:

On the night of February 21, 1961, I had a dream that actually came true—twenty-four hours later. I dreamed that my husband's brother had died, and his wife called me long distance to tell me about it.

In the dream she was crying and screaming, and I woke up terribly upset. I told my husband and later in the day, a neighbor. They both just laughed at me, and said that dreaming of a death meant a birth.

However, the next day we got the phone call. I answered. It was my sister-in-law and she was crying and screaming just *exactly* as in the dream. She said her husband had been killed that morning. He had been topping a tree and fell. *It just can't be a coincidence.* My husband has four brothers, so why should I dream about that particular one? It is so mystifying I wish I knew what caused it. (27)

In a series of clinical experiments with telepathy employing the family constellation, Schwarz noted the use of primary process mentation and dream material in the psi communication process. (28) With a thorough knowledge of family psychodynamics, he dated and charted the occurrence of telepathy in disguised everyday fashion and noted how ubiquitous the process is. Also, the close family affective bonds and the particular thematic interactional events were highlighted in a way that demonstrated the necessity of energized relationships in the transmission of psi material. Schwarz appears to be near the "transformational grammar" of the deep structure of psi language in his skillful use of the psychodynamic model. He notes repeatedly that the psi information frequently corresponds to a preconscious thought-affect on the verge of emerging from repression and entering waking consciousness.

SUMMARY

We see two factors that tend to lead to the production and recognition of spontaneously occurring psi experiences. One is intense relationships, usually of a familial and/or extremely powerful affective nature operative in the psyche of the individual. The other is reduced external input and increased "internal" sensitivity. Space and time constructions are less relevant and variable in the transmission or reception of this information. With space and time altered or oblated and the influence of powerful motivational factors occurring and manifesting in primarily unconscious ways, we see open before us the regions of dream life and sleep where perhaps continually such transactions are occurring. It should be noted that families are often sleeping at the same time and that often anecdotal data has emerged in psi material after periods of deep sleep. For that reason we plunge into that region in which we spend a third of our lives drifting.

9

The Anatomy of Sleep

The first aspect is the waking state, vaisanara. *In this state consciousness is turned to the external. With its seven instruments and nineteen channels, it experiences the gross phenomenal world.*

The second aspect is the dreaming state, taijasa. *In this state, consciousness is turned inward. It also has seven instruments and nineteen channels, which experience the subtle mental impressions.*

The third aspect is deep sleep, prajna. *In this state, there is neither desire nor dream. In deep sleep, all experiences merge into the unity of undifferentiated consciousness. The sleeper is filled with bliss and experiences bliss and can find the way to knowledge of the two preceding states.*

Mandukya Upanishad

A few hours ago you and I were in a radically different world. It came equipped with its own logic and metaphysics and honed them through imagery and energy into an existential collage of who we are. Right now the antique mahogany desk I am writing on is solid, stationary. It doesn't turn into a small cow and walk away, turning the knobs on the desk drawers into udders giving milk in the form of words and intuitions and ideas. But in a dream . . . Actually right now a third or so of us are sleeping somewhere on the planet, and of those a good percentage are actively hallucinating recurrent themes and juxtaposing situations in our orchestration of motifs and emotional dramas. Sleep moves in a pulsing wave around the planet perpetually. Dreaming, like the breath and the intuition of inner radiance, is the common tongue of our kind.

In our waking life, we are involved in two currents of perception. An outer current leads to physical things seen, heard, tasted and all combinations of these as we experience the environment. The other current moves through our mind-images, feelings, thoughts, and all such "subjective" landscapes in the genesis of experience. This outer current, this perception of external objects, voices, etc. ceases during our journey through sleep. The inner current continues on during sleep, sweeping and weaving within itself our primal energies and images that drift before the perpetual witness called the Self, and we "dream." Even dreamless sleep knows consciousness since we can have a shallow sleep or occasional bad night and thus assess the quality of our night's mentation.

Because of the profound relationship between sleep, dreaming, and psi, we can use that relationship to further the possibility of actually increasing our capacity to observe and, to a growing degree, influence that dreaming state. With that increase in observational skill, not only can we come to understand better the operation of the Family Unconscious through dreamwork, but also to realize the illusory, dreamlike quality of waking life. This technique is called *Yoga Nidra* and is similar to certain aspects of lucid dreaming. Let's look first, however, at what we currently know about the anatomy of sleep.

SLEEP AND PRATAYAHARA

It is known in the literature of sleep research that the dream cycle intervenes the sleep cycle roughly every 90 minutes. It is also noted that the sleep cycle itself has four distinct stages. (1) In the early days of experimental sleep research, it was discovered that dreaming activity could be distinguished from non-dreaming by the presence of REM or rapid eye movement during dreaming. (2) In the laboratory the researchers would awaken their subjects from sleep and ask about their mental-emotional experiences. These experiences were correlated with certain physical movements of the subjects. REM sleep tended to be highly associated with intense imagery, symbolic situations, and elaborate story form. NREM or non-rapid eye movement sleep tended to be mentation that was fragmentary, thought-like, and emotionally bland. With more sophistication, the research focused more deeply on the REM and NREM correlates of mentation and their neurophysiological concomitants. The qualitative distinction between REM and NREM has been upheld in subsequent research. (3, 4) In contrast to NREM, REM shows marked activation in several other physiological systems including heart rate, respiration, blood pressure and blood flow, brain temperature, muscular and reflex inhibition, and erection in males. There is considerable variability, however, in these autonomic indices from person to person.

The actual onset of sleep was seen to be organized into four consecutive stages involving REM and EEG (electroenphalographic electroculographic) a measure of brainwave activity. (5) These stages range subjectively from awake through drowsy to light sleep. They are: 1) alpha EEG, usually continuous, with one or more rapid eye movements a few seconds prior to the "awakenings" (Alpha REM); 2) alpha EEG, often continuous, with pronounced slow eye movements; 3) descending stage 1 EEG; and 4) descending stage 2 EEG.

The EEG has been used extensively in sleep study and other neuropsychological studies. It has some value but its results must be interpreted with caution. During the day, our brain waves are dominated by beta waves, which occupy the 18^+ to 13 hz cycle of the EEG. During states of relaxation with eyes closed or light meditation, our brain waves are characterized by a greater than usual amount of alpha wave production which occupies the 13 to 8 hz cycle of the EEG. The above-mentioned sleep states produce alpha initially. Dreaming (REM) and similar states of intense imagery and elaboration (such as hypnogogic and hypnopompic imagery) are highly associated with theta wave production, which is the 8 to 4 hz cycle. (6)

Although the reader will note varia..ons in his or her own style (researchers did note variations between subjective states of consciousness and EEG/EOG stage), there is a steady progression of stages toward sleep. In addition, with each successive stage there is a steady *decline in control* over mental activity and loss of awareness of the immediate external environment, along with an increase in frequency of hallucinatory experience. What is surprising is that mentation similar to the REM dreaming state occurred in the early sleep phase and not only in the full sleep stage. It was present half as often as in the full sleep REM. (7) While lucid dreaming or Yoga Nidra initially occurs in the low alpha, high theta range, it can be mastered at even "deeper" levels of sleep. "Below" this in deep sleep, the delta state is experienced. We are usually not conscious of mentation at the delta and some theta levels. However, certain individuals through specific meditational procedures have become "conscious" in a certain way on all these levels. (8) In Yoga Nidra the person goes into the sleep state, often by passing the dream state or else being "lucid" and self-conscious during the process. There is no loss of observational control.

We want to draw your attention to the fact that there occurs a distinct sequence of ego-awareness or observing "I" states in this process. These are even somewhat independent of EEG stages. First comes a relatively slow withdrawal from external reality, which probably facilitates the second phase. The current of perception to the outer world of objects decreases. Phase two sees the rise of regressive material or nonlogical imagery, which may actually threaten the ego since the material is not structured well and is often hallucinatory. The third is restructured or more logical material, which may be seen as an initial attempt to re-control the course of mental content. Whatever the reasons, the intact ego invariably becomes destructuralized and then quickly restructures its content. That subsystem of the psyche termed the ego is subject to certain modifications which can be observed if we can escape from the ego and perceive ourselves from a nonego perspective. Lucid dreaming and Yoga Nidra can help to lead to a holistic perception of ourselves rather than divisions into conscious, unconscious, etc.

So now let's see what actually occurs for our observing ego or "I-ness" during sleep. The waking sensory-dominated ego withdraws and re-experiences and/or restructures experiences of space and time and emotional relationships, and pays significantly less attention to external events. The inner world predominates. In these "deeper" states, space and time are reorganized when necessary and the five traditional senses may be oblated or juxtaposed. The personality system is more open to experiences within our own psyche and the psyche of others, and to psi events. These are more apt to occur as the sleeper's significant relationships are threatened, impaired, or recently activated in everyday life with great emotional intensity. Images, affects, and scenes are orchestrated by the primal energies of our nature, e.g., love, anger, pain, desire, etc. The dreaming self is an emotional self. Here psi may function as an emerging communicative system in an attempt to maintain ties to the external world which the individual has lost in sleep. Laboratory studies have established that psi does occur in dreams. Using the dream process marked by REM, Krippner, Ullman, and Vaughan (9) were able to effectively differentiate psi material in the dream content of people in the laboratory. Earlier work had labored through the methodological problems facing this kind of research.

In deep sleep, with and without dreaming, the boundaries of the observing ego undergo what Ehrenwald refers to as an "existential shift." (10) The boundaries between ego and non-ego are negotiable. In much the same way as the classical hysteric is able to dissociate certain symbolically potent areas of his or her body, e.g., an arm or leg, so it is with our egos as we go from a conscious to an unconscious level of functioning. This can readily be demonstrated with a good hypnotic subject also. That is to say, our waking ego boundaries not only are altered, but may be reconnected during the psi process in some fundamental way to another order of natural phenomena. All this occurs when our observing ego is not employing the conventional external environment and its sensory modes as a reference point. This condition of withdrawal of sensory contact with the external world has certain affinities to the state of *prataya-hara* as practiced in certain schools of meditation. After withdrawal from the external world, sensory contact is re-focused on information arising from the inner world. This inner world allows the range of the ego to grow and contact or incorporate or become part of a greater information net-work. A primitive psi has been noted to occur in this state. Other sciences such as yoga, as penetrating and empirical in their way as present-day Western science has been about the external world, have outlined the emergence of certain psi phenomena at higher levels in the pratayahara ex-perience of the inner world of consciousness. (11)

MEDITATION AND SLEEP: SOME PARALLELS

The science of *Savasana* or the art of relaxation is a milder form of withdrawal of external sensory contact. The reader can experience this when a part of the body is so relaxed that no tension is observable there. Contact with the ex-ternal world involves some level of tension. The withdrawal of all tension is initially somewhat disorienting, and in extreme cases is known as sensory deprivation. However, when the psyche has charted this inner landscape, a person is not overwhelmed by wild sensory projections.

In deep delta wave states and also extended periods of sleep, the observing ego is not only being renegotiated and modified in terms of its intimate boundaries, but it is greatly "extended." This leads to the experience of being refreshed in the morning after a "nourishing regression." Yogis have observed this state for centuries and drawn parallels.

Pratayahara, or the drawing in of the [sensory] organs, is effected by their giving up their own objects and taking, as it were, the form of the mind-stuff. The organs are separate

> stages of the mind-stuff. I see a book: the form is not in the book; it is in the mind. Something is outside which calls that form up; but the real form is in the chitta [memory]. The organs identify themselves with, and take the forms of, whatever comes to them. If you can restrain the mind-stuff from taking these forms, the mind will remain calm. (12)

Note that the observing ego does not disappear but rather is greatly expanded beyond its own capacity for self-recognition. Several scholarly Eastern researchers and yogis have described their various "awakening" experiences as vast extensions and reintegrations of their waking ego. (13) Their exact descriptions were different and indeed they practiced different methodologies, but the essential description of the dissolution and greater integration of the waking psyche are much the same. During deep sleep too, we appear to experience the dissolution of the normal waking ego, but we fail either to integrate or recognize its integration at another level of consciousness.

It should be stressed here again that the methodology employed in meditation can have a profound effect on the process. The final realization of consciousness may be identical, but the "paths" may be different. Early use of EEG with yogic meditators showed radical differences from the usual EEG of subjects. (14) The most common finding is an increase in alpha in deep meditation to the extent of blocking all other information to the system. The EEG with TM (Transcendental Meditation) showed a progressive synchronization of brain-wave activity across the whole cortex in subjects with years of steady guided practice. (15) This included not only alpha, but theta and high fast beta. (16) In earlier studies the fast beta was not noticed, but it appears to be associated with certain transcendental states. All these brain-wave patterns continually exist in all of us. It is their focus, intensity, and preponderance that is crucial.

It is to be expected that with sophistication of measuring equipment more subtle field shifts will be detected. The EEG is based on electrical measurements. A more subtle instrument, the MEG or magnetoencephlogram, is capable of detecting subtle shifts in the magnetic field of the central nervous system, thus allowing for detection of possible quantum level variations. (17, 18) This is due in part to the use of new superconducting techniques. This applied to the central and autonomic nervous systems and the chakras may open deeper realms to a consensually validating science. We indeed hope to measure and detect various energy fields associated with consciousness, using the full range of the electromagnetic spectrum, and possibly even the brain's quantum level energy fluctuations.

The observations and systems developed by many yogis indicate that the delta state, the most "quiet and slow" of the brainwave states, is the deepest state of human consciousness attained by ordinary people, and that it approaches the stage of *Turiya*. This state, Turiya, is also spoken of in the *Mandukya Upanishad*, an ancient psychological and "mystical" text on the four basic states of human consciousness: waking, dreaming, dreamless sleep, and Turiya. It is described by many as the fourth stage of human consciousness. Turiya involves a massive integration of consciousness, a transcendent perspective from which one is simultaneously aware of waking, dreaming, and NREM sleep mentation. It is beyond dreaming sleep. Yoga Nidra is more properly the state where the dreamer is conscious of his dreamsleep, but not of the outside world. Yoga Nidra involves training oneself to experience the beginning of dreaming as a coherent event that one enters, just as on waking one enters the normal ego-conscious state. Yoga Nidra is a deep meditative state which approaches Turiya, the state beyond waking, dreaming, and dreamless sleep. It is a curious phenomenon that with withdrawal of external sensory contact and as such a less aroused central nervous system, there appears to be a potentially "higher" level of consciousness.

We once thought the autonomic nervous system to be beyond the reach of consciousness, but this notion is antiquated. We know now that the dream level of mentation is also within the reach of consciousness using methods that are related to biofeedback and yoga. There is no one method of witnessing the dream state. There is no cultural monopoly on this experience. Nor is dream content the same for everyone. The artist will find it a highly visual treasure house, as did Coleridge and Stevenson, and the scientist will bring back insights on the nature of reality, which can also be cluttered in the equally symbolic/emotional world of the waking state, e.g., Edison, Kekulé. We simply note here that though dreams may seem to be symbolic processes occurring only within our own minds, sometimes they interconnect us with significant others, and at other times seem to open a door to knowledge beyond ourselves. The great yogi of Tibet Naropa even pointed out that the deepening conscious witness of this state leads to its *transformation* by way of influencing the dreamwork and our *transcendence* of the ego by so doing. Such findings prepare the ground for a fundamental insight into the operation of mind itself.

Yoga Nidra

We are again deeply indebted to Swami Rama, the yogi who helped revolutionize biofeedback by participating in research at the Menninger Foundation. (19) Swami Rama not only stopped his heart at will but demonstrated radical control over his vascular system and created delta brainwaves at will while retaining consciousness. The technique of Yoga Nidra which he teaches can lead to deeper realization and the expansion of consciousness to eventually include the dreaming state.

Yoga Nidra involves a meditation that will eventually help one see beyond the dreamwork to the similarity of dreamwork and the waking state. Both waking and dreaming involve fear, desire, etc., and are different aspects of the material/energy body. By experimenting with the dreamstate, one eventually becomes established as the witness of both dreaming and waking. The poet's intuition and the painter's canvas are fleeting glimpses into how the dream testament reflects the shared reality of both states.

When this insight occurs, it tends to affect deeply one's perception and comprehension of daily reality. While dreaming, the levels interconnect and we see how we playwrite the major characters in our emotional-ideational life. Through these observational techniques a person can better comprehend his or her own intrapsychic and Family Unconscious and become aware of the greater and lesser habits evolved in the mind.

In other words, when we are established in the state that subsumes both the waking and dreaming state, or even only briefly experience it, we see how dream and daily "reality" integrate in a meaningful pattern. Both dream and waking state are intuitively felt to be "true," and this integrated experience is the prototype of all great art. It is the dawn of what is termed the "causal level" of the mind in yogic literature, and it is reflected in great art or poetry, fusing the dream/symbol world and the logical/waking world. Art reveals to us that level of consciousness, and many worlds are seen simultaneously. The motifs and recurrent transactional energy patterns of our life can be witnessed occasionally with great benefit, not to mention the creative avenues opened to art and science. We might occasionally be conscious witness to a psi episode. This state leads to witnessing the interconnectedness of things and events, the undivided wholeness of reality as it unfolds.

One of the curious processes in dreamwork is that an image with strong emotional tone will unravel numerous other themes, all intensely interwoven. In a symbolic situation themes and images unfold from an enfolded order of patterns, intuitions, and events. Psychoanalysis relies too heavily on secondary elaboration through analyzing and discussing to grasp all the dream's manifest and latent meaning. Direct observation will lead to a *realization* or deep experience of the dream's manifold meaning, a meaning whose boundaries are not exclusively those of space, time, and causation. The mind becomes trans-spatial; time also becomes trans-temporal. Eventually, this realization emerges in the Self. Free association, etc., is but one means to observe the unfolding of the enfolded reality that interfaces with All.

A NEW PARADIGM

In these explorations we are seduced away from a paradigm which conceptualizes and identifies the *structure* of mind with the *flow* of consciousness. The psyche as an energy field with levels of relationship emerges. We begin to reorient ourselves (re-Orient!) as to the structure of the psyche and its relationship to body and consciousness. The collapse of the waking space-time categories with the dreamwork and its psi experiences leads us to this paradigm-altering perspective. We begin to see that in extraordinarily intimate ways individual psyches are connected to other psyches and often experience the same phenomena at the same time although in different places. This can be likened to a holographic or holonomic system in which each part has implicit within it each other part. It is a multileveled approach and allows us a way out of Euclidean thinking and its linear modes of causality and influence. The model has been of value in different areas of research, particularly in neurology. (20) It allows us to integrate more of the greater "field of consciousness" into our evolving conceptual schema. This extends not only to the intimate universe of the neural network, but to the external universe of physical matter. (21) The following statement by Ullman seems appropriate in this connection:

> While awake, our view of ourselves is one in which we see ourselves and stress our autonomy, our individuality, our discreteness. We define our own boundaries and we try to work with them. What I'm suggesting, and which is not at all novel, is that our dreaming self is organized along a different principle. Our dreaming self is more concerned with the nature of our connections with *all* others. There is some part of our being that has never forgotten a basic truth, that in our waking lives throughout history we seem to have continuously lost sight of. The history of the human race, while

awake, is a history of fragmentation . . . Our sleeping self, I am proposing, is concerned with the basic truth that we're all members of a single species and that while dreaming our concerns have to do with what has happened in the course of waking experience that interferes with, damages or impedes or enhances these connections. (22)

We will plunge more deeply into this sea during later chapters.

SUMMARY

What do we know of sleep, dreaming and psi? 1) That there are close affectional energies and recurrent transactional patterns operative; 2) Information exchanged is important to both sender and receiver; 3) The dream state of internal activation combined with sensory withdrawal from the external world is conducive to sharing information through imagery, intense affect and idea embedded in a mutual history of recurrent transactional patterns; 4) With practice one can enter the dream state consciously by the technique of lucid dreaming and/or Yoga Nidra.

10

Information and Transformation

*By perfectly concentrated Meditation on mind-images
is gained the understanding of the thoughts of others.*

. . . .

*By perfectly concentrated Meditation on sympathy,
compassion and kindness is gained the power of
interior union with others.*

Patanjali, Yoga Sutras

Suppose I'm not into Yoga Nidra, haven't got the energy to
invest in such techniques. What else is available for me to
directly witness the psi process as it operates through the
Family Unconscious? Is there something I can observe
while wide awake that will allow me to recognize these
events more clearly? Also, exactly what is the sequence of
events or causal network involved in this whole process?

Well, in an interesting little book entitled *The Tao of
Psychology* (1) the author, a psychiatrist, outlines many of
the situations we have previously enumerated. She har-
nesses the concept of synchronicity elucidated by Jung (2)
to support her thesis and data. In Jung's understanding of
synchronicity there is a non-causal or acausal meaningful
relationship between an inner psychic state and an external
event. There is shared meaning-image in the internal and
external world. If we assume or realize the unity of all
things, the undivided wholeness of reality, we can see how
the internal and external complement each other.

Bolen presents to us a vivid, waking, dreamlike quality of

experience such as "lucid dreaming" mentioned earlier, in which the dreamer is aware that he or she is dreaming. (In a vivid dream this element of self-consciousness is absent.) There is also an intense fusion and operation of cultural-family symbols and personal mythology in synchronous events. The "meaningfulness" of the intense dream or dreamlike waking experience in psi is taken as a measure of its authenticity.

There are at least four major types of verification of such data: 1) empirical, resting on observation of objects, and the assumption of causality; 2) logical, deriving from internal consistency and deductive reasoning; 3) experiential, stemming from direct encounter with the object or feeling, such as when the artist suddenly "finds" the right images or the lover first falls in love; 4) realization, stemming from a certain intuitive identification with the object or event. Each level has its own proof.

The author points out, just as Schmeidler did earlier, that those more open in a boundary sense to such information are more likely to "see" and recognize it than "goats" or skeptical observers. This is greatly enhanced when waking sensory stimuli are quieted or withdrawn, as is partially the case in sleep and more fully so in *pratayhara*. Bolen, the psychotherapist, also notes that the awareness of such information appears to be intimately related to feelings and affective states strongly associated to the "heart," i.e., to affective states expressing union, compassion, and empathy. This emotional vector is critical to our thinking and experience here.

Our experience of the psi sequence from earlier examples now begins to organize itself in the following process of a family-psi interaction: An event occurs to at least one member of a family in a network and the event is affectively very powerful. In this affectively-charged event—someone about to die or be injured, a visit or sensory communication with an emotionally important person who hasn't been seen in a long time, etc.—powerful patterns or themes of interaction are reactivated. In this interaction between family members an archetypal situation occurs and is reflected in the way they interact. This can be the "nurturing relationship," or intimates in a compassionate/lover relationship, or any other style of relationship that humans have experienced collectively through thousands of years of shared experience. These patterns are embedded in the matrix of human experience. There is an interface between individual or family systems that create or participate in the larger field or system of humanity. The point of interaction *includes* both other systems, and there is information exchange between psyches separated by space. The Euclidean "space" between distant psyches is somehow bent or convoluted, certainly altered, and the possibility therein exists for "time" to undergo a fundamental alteration. Space-time becomes fluid. The personal or individual unconscious is activated by the emotional energy of a powerful constellation of events, and this inner network of affect, patterns, and events reflects his or her relationships within the matrix of family events and the Family Unconscious.

These relationships, in turn, occur as a reflection of events occurring in the system of the collective unconscious of humanity at large. This is not to say that one system *causes* the events in the others. Rather, they occur simultaneously as a manifestation of ultimate interconnectedness. Energy and information are exchanged in a "supraluminal" way, which means moving faster than the speed of light. "Luminous" means moving at the speed of light. "Subluminal" means moving below the speed of light, the rate at which material "objects" manifest. At and above the speed of light causality is radically transformed.

We realize that the above formulation requires some shift in our understanding of causality. Yet we have to point out that conventional perceptions of causality are related to body boundary experiences, which are deeply rooted in our earliest mental constructions, as Piaget has amply demonstrated. (3, 4) This forms the basis of one of our principal difficulties in accepting such phenomena in the "rational" sense. Experiencing such events validates them beyond rational validation.

PSYCHE: FOCUS AND FIELD

Now in order for psi information to occur and be recognized, the energy fields of the individuals involved must be harmonious, or in phase sequence. In other words, there needs to be a coherence "across" and "within" the patterns. Intimate contact and emotional coherence where two people feel the same thing at the same time, such as in the mother-child symbiosis, are conducive to psi, as are similar emotionally powerful situations where certain interactions have recurred over and over. In such instances psi is often registered below the threshold of awareness on a subliminal level with psychophysiological correlates, as we saw in Dean's research. (5, 6) It was noted earlier that in sleep the observing ego attends less to external stimuli and more attention is directed toward primary process and affectively powerful material. In this process the observer undergoes radical changes. The autonomic nervous system also receives greater attention during sleep, and the other senses and space and time categories are renegotiated. It is quite possible that some other center in the body such as the solar plexus (called by some the "other brain") affects consciousness and is implicated in the autonomic nervous system. (7)

We have seen that there are different levels of awareness for the observing ego. It seems reasonable that there may also be levels of consciousness in the psyche beyond those available to the ego. Psychodynamic theory has no difficulty with the conscious, preconscious, and unconscious levels of the psyche's operations. We merely extend the model on both "ends" to include the family and collective unconscious on one end and the superconscious (8) or level of highest intuition and inspiration on the other. For psi to occur these various levels of consciousness and energy operative within and through the psyche need to come into a phase-coherence relationship with other psyches under specific conditions outlined above. It is helpful to hold in abeyance the question of whether the psyche is located totally *in* the physical brain. Many other viable models of brain-mind functioning are available to experiment with such that our data acquires a neater fit. (9, 10) One promising model to explore is that of other levels or "energy shells" around the individual psyche. We will go into this in the next chapter, along with the normal waking-ego consciousness. For now, it will suffice to note that the familial patterns of interaction and affective energy shells around certain recurrent themes leads to an energy-information exchange during phase sequence. The family members create certain "resonate affinities" with each other that therein become the "frequency" or interface points of transmission.

At times the psyche appears to us to operate as an open field with networks of influence and mutual formation. It is then in a sense expansive, relaxed, cholinergic. In non-ego dominated conditions it "connects" with other psyches. It has, if you will, a certain wave/field character at such times. At other times the psyche seems contracted, tensed, adrenergic, and focused. It has, if you will, a focus point or discrete particle aspect to its character. The psyche, over duration and in different conditions, seems to expand and contract, and show the dual manifestation of particle and wave. It literally "pulses" at certain energy levels, which result from certain recurrent transactional patterns with high levels of affective charge. Various members of the system appear to share these "frequency" or energy levels which operate *through* and *within* each individual psyche. This field comprises a matrix in which psyches at times appear to be separate points emerged from the field and at other times are completely identified with the field.

It therefore appears to us that the Family Unconscious, the field of relationships with strong emotional charge, has certain established interactional patterns between its "focus" points or individual members. These resonate affinities are constantly interacting with each other. The principle of resonance absorption is helpful here in providing a model that operationally conceptualizes this issue. In this model we can fleetingly see how an aspect of one field is taken in or emitted by an aspect of another field with similar structural properties. Thus in resonance absorption it seems that "in every frequency band (or for specific frequencies within a band) there exists one or more natural or manmade resonators that *absorb* within that frequency band . . . the effects produced by the energy absorbed by a particular resonator depend on the *characteristics* of the resonator." (11) The interaction of electromagnetic radiations with matter is basically similar although different materials are affected at different wavelengths. The resonating structure thus determines the radiation which will affect it. (12) We exist in a matrix of resonating frequencies and structures. If we listen closely, a certain harmony will emerge.

11

Chakras and Affective Currents

What seems to me particularly important about the discovery that "energy levels" are virtually nothing but the frequencies of normal modes of vibration is that now one can do without the assumption of sudden transitions, or quantum jumps, since two or more normal modes may very well be excited simultaneously . . . one must give up entirely the idea of the exchange of energy in well-defined quanta and replace it with the concept of resonance between vibrational frequencies . . . we can no longer consider the individual particle as a well-defined permanent entity.

E. Schrödinger, What Is Matter

I am You and You are Me and We are all together. Right Now.

The Beatles, Magical Mystery Tour

We are moving closer to an understanding of how information can be transmitted at a distance through psi. We have seen how families develop deeply entrenched themes and modes of interaction, and that these persist as children grow and families develop. It is not unreasonable to assume that these themes, which become very energetic through constant repetition and emotional charge, take on the likeness of a transmission system. If this is so, then we might expect family members to resonate to "frequencies" set up by these themes which would underlie information transfer.

Here again we must borrow from known models to help, but again must take care not to confuse the map with the actual territory.

Modern science is comfortable with "levels" of interactions and hierarchical schemas. The early Bohr atom was seen as having orbits at different distances from the nucleus. This was later modified by the notion of quantum energy shells at discrete levels around and through the nucleus. In other words, an electron will move, not just anywhere, but only at certain distances or energy levels from the nucleus in a series of orbits or "energy shells." The move from one level to another appears disjointed or discrete, as if the "space" between levels had somehow been bypassed. The field looks discrete here, yet at other times appears continuous, as in Relativity theory.

We use this merely as an analogy to the different levels of consciousness or mentation. In Chapter 6 we saw that yoga describes fields emanating from the human organism at different levels or "frequencies"—the *pranamaya kosha* with vitality feeding the physical body, the *manomaya kosha* composed of mental energies, etc. These fields and the conscious states associated with them can be compared to "energy shells" that jump in "frequency" from one level to another in quantum leaps. We use this as an analogy to highlight our experience of levels of interaction around and through the psyche. We can see how in chemical bonding at least the outer electron shell connects with the outer electron shells of other atoms to form a whole unit in a molecule. Later we will see how in the interior of the atom the subatomic particles "share" energy and identity. For now we can see how, analogously, these levels or shells in us at times are shared by other "atomic" entities, that is, other people, and psi occurs.

It is interesting to see how in the atomic structure an orbiting particle going from one energy level to another in a shell absorbs or emits a certain quantum of energy. The analogy to levels of consciousness, especially in meditation, is striking. We know that we can affect subtle neurophysiological aspects of our system just by consciousness, as in biofeedback and hypnosis and also in highly creative and transcendent states. This ability supports the idea of higher levels of mentation interacting with the physical.

These fields or levels which interpenetrate the body would appear to be associated with discrete energy locations within the human body-organization. The autonomic nervous system contains a system of nerve plexuses which affect higher and lower levels of consciousness. There are plexuses or nerve bundles located along the spine at discrete intervals. These are the collection of nerve endings of both the sympathetic and parasympathetic branches. Each of these plexuses has an integrating capacity to coordinate various nerve impulses and is involved in specific functions, such as the anal, the genitourinary, the digestive system, circulation, the respiratory system. The higher centers involve the autonomic nervous system and hormone system of the whole body, as well as the central nervous system and all the organs and tissues. These plexuses are associated with psychic centers, *chakras* in yogic terminology. Each is also associated with a certain set of emotions, psychophysiological activities and, very importantly, with specific modes of perception and consciousness. The chakras are situated over the nerve plexuses, but they occur in the various levels of the organism's fields, not in the physical body itself.

At each plexus the nerve endings of the sympathetic and parasympathetic nervous system do not touch but rather intermingle. These nerve endings, like all nerves, have an electric current of low voltage running through them. It is well known that an electric current generates a magnetic field around it, and this subtle field appears to be operative at the plexuses. "Passive attention" as demonstrated in biofeedback and meditation employs very little energy and could potentially interact with these subtle fields. This occurs when consciousness is focused, for instance, at a particular location in the body. Chanting a specific mantra or sound vibration may serve to amplify the subtle field at each plexus. According to some traditions, these specific sounds or vibrations, when consciously focused, will resonate with and activate these vibrational centers. (1) This must be done only with a *personal* teacher and with care or one may experience extreme unpleasantness at a certain stage in one's practice.°

In a series of experiments, Motoyama indirectly measured the variation of the electromagnetic field around specific plexus or chakras when subjects were consciously focusing on these areas. (2, 3) He set up electrode plates opposite each chakra. Changes in the field were amplified by standard electronic equipment as the energy emanated from the chakra across the electrode plates. He found that meditation on a chakra can be shown to deflect the electromagnetic field around that chakra. (This is similar to the early detection of subatomic particles by deflection of its pathway and use of the inferential process.) Significant differences were found between subjects depending on which chakra they focused on and how many years they had spent in meditation on that site. Motoyama believes these energies are the Ki energy of the subtle body used in

---

°We mention this here because as the seeker uses various procedures and opens to "higher" realms, the "lower" realms also open. In the integration of the consciousness, both experiences occur, as Aurobindo has repeatedly stressed. These lower realms include our prehuman experience, which means our mammalian and reptilian ancestry. In the collective unconscious these occur at critical periods in a culture's history. Note the ancient Mayans and their worship of the serpent in their science/religion. It was both a high point of their advanced civilization and a contact with lower realms (W. I. Thompson's "Assent of the Serpent," *Re-Vision*, Fall/Winter 1982). It was an attempt at the integration of wisdom/intuition and the lower reptilian. In our own day, late 1970s and 1980s, we note the fusion of such in culturally popular art forms (movies) which, because of their mass psychological appeal, do express the collective unconscious. Both Yoda and E. T., the Extra Terrestial, are compassion/wisdom/intuition figures with reptilian lineages. The science of Kundalini Yoga is familiar with this.

acupuncture. Monitoring the anahata chakra or heart area of one advanced subject, Motoyama was able to register the activation of a photo-electric cell. Energy has also been detected being emitted from other energy centers in the body. This is interesting in connection with Inyushin's bioplasmic activity hypothesis and the emission of photons in bioluminescence not caused by high temperature.

We think of these plexuses as resonate vibrational centers in the systems of higher and lower orders of consciousness. They are nexuses of energy and information. These centers are capable of interaction with each other. They are characterized by a certain inward- and outward-flowing propensity.

An uncanny finding has been uncovered in a series of classical experiments carried out by the Swiss scientist Hans Jenny. (4) Dr. Jenny, in exploring the inner structure of sound, vibrated different substances at particular frequencies of sound. He then photographed the vibrations that resulted, like photographing an echo reverberating through a canyon. His instrument, called a "tonoscope," demonstrated that the tone of the ancient seed mantra OM uttered into a microphone created the visual pattern of a certain yantra or meditational mandala used by the ancient Hindus.° The syllable OM produced a circle which was then filled in with concentric squares and triangles. Here modern Western technology revealed an exact correspondence of inner directed conscious vibration and external visual representation. One has to put a great deal of faith in chance and randomness to account for this in terms of a coincidence.

°This yantra, termed *Sri Yantra*, is known in the Samaya Tantric tradition to be a symbol of the law of manifestation or physical vibratory expression in matter, and is the root or mother of all vidyas or symbols, the Sri Vidya. The worlds within worlds symbolized are particularly interesting from a holonomic universe perspective. In other words, each triangulated figure is implicated in each other figure, and they all unfold out toward the limits of the whole figure, and conversely enfold into each other toward the center.

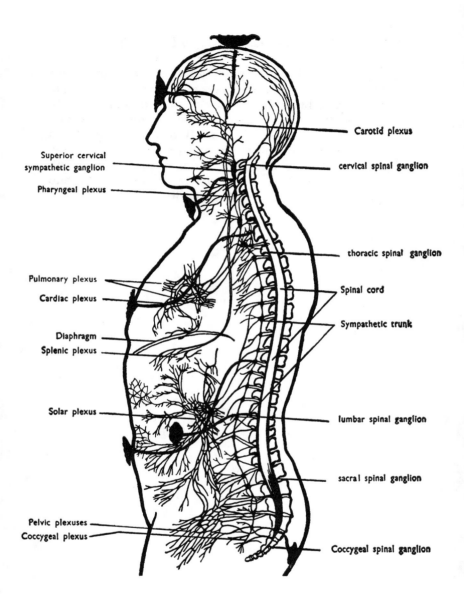

Carotid plexus

Superior cervical sympathetic ganglion

cervical spinal ganglion

Pharyngeal plexus

thoracic spinal ganglion

Pulmonary plexus

Cardiac plexus

Spinal cord

Sympathetic trunk

Diaphragm

Splenic plexus

Solar plexus

lumbar spinal ganglion

sacral spinal ganglion

Pelvic plexuses

Coccygeal plexus

Coccygeal spinal ganglion

The Chakras and the Nervous System

The seven chakras or psychic centers and the body's autonomic nerve plexuses (from C. W. Leadbeater, *The Chakras*, Wheaton, IL. Theosophical Publishing House, 1980, p. 40).

Our sense is that the energy generated at each plexus involves subtle, high frequencies of the type known as the biogravitational field. These fields can be detected, amplified, directed, and are capable of information transfer. The reader is referred back to Section III for a fuller exploration of bioplasma and the biogravitational field. Suffice it to say that each of us, including the reader at this very moment, has each chakra and plexus active at some lower and occasionally higher degree of intensity.

12

Chakras and Family Motifs

The pattern of reciprocity in family role relations, man to wife, father to mother, parent to child, influences in a fundamental way the vicissitudes of personal conflict and the fate of individual psychopathological symptoms.
    N. Ackerman, The Psychodynamics of Family Life

We mentioned earlier that associated with each chakra are specific emotional/psychological energies and aspects of consciousness. Jung, of course, recognized these levels but only dimly. Joseph Campbell has catalogued the motifs of numerous cultural symbols, myths, and traditions which characterize these levels of consciousness. (1) A fuller description of the chakras and plexuses can be found in Leadbeater (2) and the postulated personality repercussions of each in Rama et al. (3)

The information available about chakras can be related to Louisa Rhine's work on spontaneous cases of psi, which indicated that despite the numerous situations and contents of psi, only a few general themes emerged, with the family central. We will now explore how these different emotional/psychological constellations are embedded in specific family transactional styles. We will look into the interior of the Family Unconscious.

FAMILY MOTIFS

The family whose themes are developed around issues of survival, emotional or physical, with a low trust level and high hostility are not likely to transmit psi information, much less receive it. Threats in such families are not sensed so much as merely presenting the danger of loss but of potential total psychological annihilation. The insecurity created by transactional patterns in such a family occasionally erupts in psychosis and the paranoid style. More often latent fear and distrust ("ontological insecurity") pervades the development of the psyches in this family constellation. Rama and others hold that this kind of emotional energy level is associated in the yogic chakra system with the first level or root chakra level termed the *muladhara*. It is highly charged with concern for biological survival, fears of injury, of attack and being attacked, and is embedded in potentiality in each psyche as a consequence of its use in an earlier period of evolutionary need. Note the emotional connection between intense fear and defecation and the anatomical position of this chakra. It is likely that the world view of one who focuses primarily at this level is hyper-materialistic, emphasizing the "hard facts." The collective myths such as slaying dragons, etc., may originate here. It is perhaps the "denser" aspect of our being.

A family whose interactional themes are often centered around issues of rivalry, sexual competition, and to some extent sensuality, are slightly more likely to employ psi for information transfer. This is because such families have occasional periods of tenderness and slightly less ego-defensiveness. Swami Rama and his associates place this at the second level associated with genitourinary functioning. For anyone mostly focused at this level, the swadhistana chakra, people are seen very much as objects, sexual objects. In contrast to the first, its themes allow more creativity, less rigidity in roles, but it is still fairly inflexible. Freud may have operated out of this framework.

The third or *manipura* chakra is characterized by a world view that emphasizes domination and submission. Psi information is more expressible at this level than lower levels due to greater periods of closeness and intimacy, even though these are hampered by oppressive power dynamics. The constellation and interaction of families at this level frequently center on issues of power and authority. The ego defenses of such persons are structured to deal with constant struggling with powerful others, and only domination or submission roles are acceptable. Such individuals are often referred to as authoritarian personalities. Perceived from this energy-consciousness level, other individuals are seen as either superior or inferior, as either authority figures or underlings, not peers. Note that this chakra is associated with the digestive system. Psychological studies of ulcer patients show that they are often the sort of people who force themselves to take on the responsibilities of a dominant, controlling position, although basically they have a tendency to be passive, dependent, and submissive. Ulcers demonstrate anatomically the conflict characteristic of this level.

The Dawn of Psi

The beginning of significant numbers of psi information events occurs with the fourth or *anahata* chakra level of interaction, in the area of the heart. When this level is the focus, there may be an intensification of earlier primal union relationships, e.g., mother-child symbioses or intense lover relationships. Also at this level there can be a full loss of individual ego-defensiveness in true altruism and compassion. Family interactions here are characterized not by loss of identity in fusion relationships, but by a true "communicative intimacy." (4) This is an open, steady-state system. There is the experience of great "observing ego" expansion upon meditation at this level, in addition to increased psi exchanges. Motoyama has experimented with such energy fields and also finds that while psi can occur at level three, the level of dominance-submission, that there is a dramatic increase in instances of psi at the fourth level. (5, 6) This finding is corroborated by Bolen when she emphasizes that compassion is highly correlated with psi information of various kinds. The work of Murphy is replete with cases in which the intimate empathetic relationship of families and individuals coincides with the occurrence of psi information events. (7) The recurrent transactional patterns of this type of family are around themes of genuine openness, a great deal of unconditional positive regard, and compassion. Numerous instances of psi show the heart level or compassion-altruism level. Note in the following psi exchange the family dynamics and the "heart" center of the anahata chakra:

> Two years ago my parents went away on a short vacation. Shortly after they left on their trip my small son became very ill and had an extremely high temperature. Early the next morning I was surprised to see my parents driving into the driveway. Mother rushed in and said, "I had a terrible dream. I dreamed I kissed Billy and he was burning with fever and when I turned around John (my brother) was standing there with a big hole in his head, pouring blood." I told her that Billy was terribly sick but that my brother John had gone to work as usual that morning and was just fine. In less than an hour my brother, a lineman for Southern Bell Telephone Company, had been brought home by his foreman with a big hole cut above his left eye, and bleeding profusely. (8)

In the therapist-client relationship it is quite possible that the third level, that of power and manipulation, is operative to some degree in addition to the fourth. We want to point out that at any time several chakras or vibrational centers may be active. But for psi to occur, the higher must be active. In case of death or accident, the root chakra is involved because of issues of survival, but the fourth must be receptive to the process.

The fifth chakra, termed the *vishuddha*, is situated in the throat near the thyroid gland which regulates the metabolism of food and the use of oxygen. This center is highly associated, therefore, with nurturance. It is an area of receiving, which includes caring for others and giving care, a certain sense of trust, and connection with the source of these. In psychoanalytic theory the first hunger for nurturance and creativity comes in the oral stage. Here it can be seen as the search for help, growth, development.

One at this stage wants to take in the world, to merge with the loving and nurturant source of things. It is the focus of vocalization, of singing, of verbalization, and again of creativity. We are not focusing on the pathological aspects but on the creative and uniquely human aspect of language and symbolization.

The family whose themes predominate or are markedly influenced at this level interact around creativity as a valued part of their life. Sometimes families produce artists for generations. Art is an aspect of the Family Unconscious of that system, and open support for creativity and searching is evident in its members.

Few families function at the level of the sixth chakra, the ajna, as this is a most highly developed and rare level of functioning. Although occasionally in clinical practice one comes across a family where many of the members evidence psi capacity and consciously employ it, few families stress the open value of deep, "intuitive" knowledge which is associated with this chakra. It is situated slightly above the eyes at the space between the eyebrows. It is opposite the *muladhara* chakra in the sense that it is the least "dense" of the chakras except for the uppermost chakra. In folk legend it is referred to as the "third eye" or seat of intuitive knowledge. Interestingly enough, it is located very near the pineal gland, which was thought by the ancients to be sensitive to "a light within." Descartes even located the mind-body interchange here. Recently, however, it has been demonstrated that the pineal gland, despite being deep in the skull, is sensitive to light. Though not directly connected to the external environment, it does respond to daily and seasonal patterns of light. (9) This level is also spoken of as allowing insights that transcend or oblate the usual space-time coordinates.

Above this is the highest chakra, the *sahasrara*, the experience of which is beyond any verbal or mental description. It is located in the top-center of the head and its plexus is the cerebral cortex which governs all our systems. No family dynamics other than seeking and supporting transcendence are operative here.

Clearly not all interactions in a family are dominated by the same level, and indeed many levels are influential in a family constellation of transactions, just as they are in the individual psyche. However, certain patterns do emerge as primary and characterize family styles. They occur and are participated in through the personal intrapsychic and Family Unconscious. Energies from these patterns are being generated all the time into the holonomic sea about us. We have suggested that phase coherence between energy levels within this larger field of relationships leads to the psi exchange. This exchange is always embedded in an archetypal constellation of events in an affectively charged matrix.

Research and observations indicate that families and family-affective interactions generally operate at the first, second, and third levels we have outlined. Level four occurs in more open, flexible families. Other levels occur more rarely in individuals and families, but clearly they do occur, and just as importantly, can be observed and amplified. The enormous possibilities for healing are beyond our present imagination. One has only to see successful family therapy in operation to witness the immense power of released "positive" and "negative" energy on an individual and a system.

In the Afrocentric world view, which has spread to most areas in the Western world, especially South America and the Caribbean, the family influence on health and illness is well recognized. The question often asked by the therapist/healer with this view is not "what" is the matter with you, but "who" is the matter with you. (10) The present-day school of family therapists is actually operating out of the same paradigm, although they use different metaphors.

CONSCIOUSNESS AND ENERGY

A word on models in closing. We have used, for heuristic or problem-solving purposes, both the quantum model of levels of energy relationship and the yogic model of levels of consciousness. We have also borrowed when necessary from other frames of reference. These are only models to aid us in our conceptualization and should not be taken as an exact correspondence. Otherwise we succumb to the fallacy of misplaced concreteness. The territory is not the map. We do not completely *identify* consciousness with energy. They occur together, but in our understanding they are different. Consciousness itself is understood to be wholly outside the realm of matter and energy but is also wholly co-extensive with it. Insofar as psi involves energy transfer, we see three factors involved: consciousness, the energy field, and the information. *Consciousness* introduces the *information* into the *energy field*, and the energy field then transmits the information. The information itself is quite other than the energy used to transmit it, just as words are not electrical activity in a phone wire. This is why consciousness remains the great mystery. As mentioned earlier, we avoid identifying the *structure* of mind with the *flow* of consciousness. We see the psyche or affective field of an individual participating in consciousness but distinct from consciousness itself. Ask yourself how it is that yogis and mystics have perceived the "highest" energy fields. If the eye cannot see itself, neither can the "highest" energy field be that which perceives itself. Nor can that energy field introduce into itself the information of psi. A psi transmission appears to require some higher-order influence to introduce or impose a controlling and directive order upon the transmission medium. That higher-order influence is seen to be consciousness, and the transmission medium is seen to be the affective energy fields we have outlined. This is a subtle distinction but an important one.

The next chapter will focus on personal and clinical experiences of the author in the operation of psi.

13

The Family Unconscious
in Day-to-Day Life

*The relationship of the unconscious of the therapist to
the unconscious of the patient underlies any therapy.
This provides the ultimate in depth, the ultimate in
experience and, as such, must be both quantitatively
and qualitatively the common denominator of therapy.*
C. Whitaker, The Roots of Psychotherapy

Jogging along the pavement or a back country road, we
become aware of nature all around us, including that nature
that moves in our breath and sweat as we run. As we feel the
muscle and sinew, we sense that heat and water economized
in the run slowly unfolds the capacity of the body. But if we
watch from a passing car having never jogged ourselves, all
this description is less than theory.

Experience and empirical science issue from direct
observation and to some degree predictability. Actual
manipulation may or may not be an aspect of each area of
study. Astronomy is a science, yet no one manipulates the
stars. The two great functions of a theory are, first, to serve
as a *tool* whereby direct empirical investigation is facili-
tated and, second, to *organize* and *order* empirical knowledge and deepen understanding of natural phenomena.
This involves some prediction and some replication.

Psi is an area that has been notorious for lack of replication. Earlier chapters have sought to show that some psi
studies have been replicated in the lab. These, of course,

help us better to see psi in life and in the clinical situation. The final chapter of this section will go deeper into the interior of the psi process and examine the data such that the *general conditions* of the psi occurrence are more observable in context. Within the field dynamics of your own life, you can begin to make observations and rudimentary predictions. Remember that the mind's dynamics are more akin to innumerable, interconnecting waves and images that float under a bridge than to the fixed, solid bridge itself.

Below we will outline four observations and from them indicate what can be predicted. Two are taken from the clinical setting; the other two come from everyday life. They will progressively reveal more of the intimate emotional context which is at the nerve-root of the psi experience. In each example there is embedded the constellation we have previously elaborated: family-energy roles of individuals with their affective charges; an emotional state of empathy of *anahata*/heart chakra at that moment; a shared history of recurrent transactional patterns; one individual being in a focused or adrenergic state while the other is in a very relaxed or cholinergic state. They will fall into two modes of interaction:

A. A husband and wife, lovers, or close friends who experience some true *empathy* and *intimacy* with each other. One is relaxed, e.g., resting, dreaming, etc., the other is mentally concentrating on a problem or such. At these times we can observe a higher incidence of simultaneous thoughts, mutual associations, and a spontaneous concurrence of previously unverbalized intentions between them. Sometimes this occurs when both are dreaming and one is highly emotional.

B. In the clinical setting where the psychotherapist and client share a history of transactional patterns, an affectively charged, positive and psychologically rich relationship called transference and counter-transference, and while the therapist listens with relaxed, free-floating attention (cholinergia) to the client's release of affect (adrenergia) one can observe an increase in similarities in recent events and emotions that both have experienced. These often involve the dreamlife of both client and therapist. Insight into the patient may suddenly deepen. The therapist is engaged by way of his or her own intense interest or unresolved conflict in the affective complex. The transference and counter-transference provide the affective current for such information exchange.

CASE HISTORIES

1. On a Friday in Feburary I awoke refreshed from sleep, did my Sadhana (meditation) and went to work at the University's health service clinic. At 9 a.m. I was asked to come down the hall into the main office by Dr. Kent Poey. There I found a birthday cake for me for my 35th birthday. Since I was not coming in on Monday, Friday was the day to celebrate this at the office with the staff. The senior clerk receptionist, Shelli M., was going to turn 25 on the same day I was to turn 35. We had shared birthdays at work for several years now and had affectionately talked about it over the last few weeks.

I enjoyed myself and then put it out of consciousness in order to work with my patients. My 11 o'clock patient, Peter C., came in and was upset and depressed. I consciously relaxed in order to hear him fully. I liked Peter very much and identified with his strong interest in science. During the course of the session he discussed the erratic, painful dissolution of his passionate love affair. He mentioned this out of the blue in connection with his 27th birthday, which had just occurred. The woman told him of her new "lover" on his birthday [sic].

Suddenly I remembered a very similar constellation of events with similar dynamics had occurred to me during my 27th year as I prepared for my birthday. As in Peter's situation, a certain aspect of low self-esteem and personality dynamics was played out in a relationship. During this time in the session, Peter C. was agitated (adrenergia) and I felt empathic but relaxed and observing my primary process (cholinergia). Peter C. even noted at the end of the session my deep and "beyond professional" feeling for him during this particular session.

Note: a) states of activation and relaxation of "sender" and "receiver," i.e., adrenergia and cholinergia; b) "family" atmosphere of affect between Shelli M., me, and my patient, especially empathy; c) counter-transference of therapist is implicated; 3) archetypal event of birthdays as part of interpersonal dynamics.

2. On a September day my wife Alyse and I went to visit with William B. and Cathy K. at the place where William and I had completed our internships in psychology, he his pre-doctoral and me my post-doctoral. Alyse and I met only three months before I met William. Cathy and William themselves were to be married. We all felt like good old friends who shared history, affects, and certain events together.

It was late afternoon when we stopped at an antique shop. Alyse spied two old copies of Time Magazine, the September 22, 1947, issue with Jackie Robinson on the cover, and the July 1, 1946, issue with Albert Einstein on the cover. We thought them interesting and that they would go well on an antique table for our living room. We made a joke about the juxtaposition of Black and Jewish themes on the covers, a dynamic that was implicated in our own marital/cultural psychodynamics. As we were driving away, it occurred to me to see who the magazines had originally been mailed to. I looked down and saw that they were both originally shipped to:

> William J. Van Beynum
> Travelers Insurance Co.
> Albany, N.Y.

Here in the address was my own name, Bynum, and my middle initial, J for Joseph, as well as William B.'s first name! We all noted with excitement that this was synchronicity. It was only later that we noted that this occurred in the anniversary week of William's and my seven-year history as friends. We had met on the 2nd of September, 1975, and the day was the 4th of September, 1982.

Note: a) "family" feeling and Family Unconscious affective matrix, especially "brotherly" affect of myself and William; Black and Jewish themes; shared history of relationship and transactional patterns around empathy; b) similarity of names in address of magazines; William and J., but also the names of Beynum, Bynum, and Williams' last name of Boylin; c) *relaxed*, open emotional state of the party as we perused the antique shop (cholinergia?); d) *anniversary* nature of event as archetypal event, i.e., 7th year meeting in autumn up the road from our initial confluence.

3. After a sleep-filled night in December, my wife and I mentioned our dreams to each other, as is our custom. I had dreamed a strange dream in which a "grandmother type" was trying to reach or catch me. She had "mixed feelings" of protection and also somehow of "getting me." Also in the dream the "grandmother type" attempted to steal or cut-off a pickle I had! Having a somewhat Freudian lens, I made note of the sexual aspect of this. I later woke up with a slightly eerie feeling about the dream, but not tired.

On the same night my wife Alyse dreamed of my grandmother (L. G.) who had a necklace with a moon-shaped crescent locket. The locket fell partly from her neck but not completely, and turned into a knife or sharp edge. Alyse then wondered in the dream, because of the shape and opening up of the locket as it hung around my grandmother's neck, whether the grandmother was "gay." Note the correspondence of grandmother images, sexual feeling, and cutting. Neither of us had discussed grandmothers for a long, long time and we could remember no events recently that would account for the dream in terms of day-residue.

4. I was in session with my patient, Michael S. I had not seen this patient since late summer, but before that we met weekly for several months. I had the counter-transference feeling of slight dismay at this patient coming back for "therapy again," and I was a little put off. My sense and image of myself as a "good therapist," however, was in

executive position with the ego, and so I saw him for the hour.

During the hour I occasionally drifted away but would catch myself being slightly bored (cholinergia?) and bring my attention back to full focus on him. At a certain point while listening to Michael S. most of the time, I noticed a familiar rocking motion at the base of my spine and a gently flowing movement. I had first acquired this movement (kriya) that summer at Muktananda's ashram in South Fallsburg, New York. Then the rocking would occur with more or less intensity during my morning Sadhana or yoga practice.

During this particular session my attention drifted back and forth from this rocking in the spine, always gentle and relaxing, to my patient. I then began to listen closely to my "primary process," and suddenly there appeared the image of the patient as a little boy. This was partially because of the present conversation. We were talking of family matters (Family Unconscious) and he was affectively relating the details.

The image I had was of the patient as a little boy being forced to push a porcupine quill up his behind! After making sure that this was not my own wish or projection, I trusted my intuition and shared my "off the wall" image with him. He became even more alert and spoke of a powerful image he carried with him as a little boy. It was even part of his dreamlife, but he had not thought of it for years (M. S. was 23 years old and only a sophomore). His image was of a pencil always thrust up his behind! This image and affect then led to more of an exploration of his family, self pressures, parental divorce conflicts, and his painful learning disability of dyslexia since childhood and the family's emphasis on professional and academic achievement. It opened up a formerly sleepy session.

Note: a) The shared unconscious image was *similar*. b) I am in the relaxed state of *cholineria*. c) Patient is in the affective state of *adrenergia*. d) Discussion of session at the moment was *family matters*, e.g., Family Unconscious and

affective currents. e) Counter-transference of the therapist
is involved, i.e., therapist felt that client was perhaps being
"thrust up" his "behind" by returning for "therapy again."
f) Psi process began as a diffuse image on the boundary of
the observing ego in primary process and free association,
leading to a clearer reflection of shared imagery.

Although we disagree about the involvement of the
therapist's own Family Unconscious, a similar process has
been observed by Whitaker and Malone (1981) in the therapeutic encounter involving countertransference.

> Therapy involves an increasing accessibility of each parti-
> cipant's unconscious dynamics to the other. More
> specifically, the intra-psychic dynamics of the therapist
> involve his unconscious reactions to the patient as a pro-
> jection of himself. The intra-psychic dynamics of the
> therapist demand, primarily, the integration of his current
> feelings into his total self (body-image problem) as these are
> specifically stimulated by the projected feelings of the
> patient. Together these force the therapist to precipitate
> himself into residues of his own transference feelings. In
> short, the therapist experiences both the dynamics of his
> own body-image integration, and the vestiges of his infantile
> familial experience as these continue to be present in
> residual as his 'intra-psychic family.' The intra-psychic
> dynamics of the patient involve, primarily, his reaction to
> the therapist as the latter provokes feelings specific to the
> functioning of the patient's transference needs where these
> have been previously internalized as his own intra-psychic
> family. The patient, in short, has an intra-psychic experience
> in which the therapist participates to a greater or lesser
> extent. In contrast the therapist has an essentially non-
> familial and, primarily, personal experience which deals
> with the relationship of his various 'parts' to his inte-
> grated wholeness. (1)

We would extend this field of experience and mutually
influencing process to incorporate it into other laws of
energy dynamics. The "energy" field we have been
exploring manifests dynamics at various levels and under

different but identifiable conditions. This energy field is *similar* to other energy fields and interactions known in nature. It is similar to the gravitational force in that it appears to be primarily attractive in nature; similar to both the gravitational and electromagnetic forces in "infinite" range and possibly the "exchange" of massless "information" particles; similar to the "weak force" in that it is extremely difficult to detect unless we are specifically attuned to it as it appears to radiate from the organism much as the decay process of the nucleus. Its power even appears to be *similar* to the inverse square laws embedded in the electrostatic, magnetic and gravitational fields except that the "field" is holographic and the "mass" or density of the "objects" is a function of affective-ideational intensity.

If we were to clinically formulate the psi episode, it would be something like the following: The deepest aspect of the human being, which we will call the Self, locates an aspect of itself in the Self of another. The two share the field of the Family Unconscious. That shared field becomes energized by the occurrence of an archetypal event to one of the persons. The whole process is then mediated and "transmitted" by the power or magnitude of the biogravitational energy of a specific group of autonomic nervous system plexuses or chakras. Each variable in the system fluctuates in degree of intensity until the particular constellation of variables reaches a critical point, at which time the psi episode transpires. This psi episode is a discontinuous or discrete process despite the fact that the variables are in continuous change from one stable state to another stable state.

The psi process and its energy system share certain qualities with the other presently known forces or interactions of nature. Yet psi is also implicated in natural forces we know much less about. This enigma draws us toward a deeper look at these so called "fundamental forces" of the universe. This vast and intricate field interfaces the firing of a neuron and the collapse of a star.

V

Toward a New Paradigm: Psi, Physics, Psychology, and the Self

Therefore, any theory which tries to fulfill the require-ments of both special relativity and quantum theory will lead to mathematical inconsistencies, to divergen-cies in the region of very high energies and momenta.
        Heisenberg, Physics and Philosophy

Each theory is committed to its own notions of es-sentially static and fragmentary modes of existence (relativity to that of separate events, connectable by signals, and quantum mechanics to a well-defined quantum state). One thus sees that a new kind of theory is needed . . . rather an entirely different sort of basic connection of elements is possible, from which our ordinary notions of space and time, along with those of separately existent material particles, are abstracted as forms derived from a deeper order.
        Bohm, Wholeness and the Implicate Order

. . . the body is not mere unconscious Matter: it is a structure of a secretly conscious Energy that has taken form in it. Itself occultly conscious, it is, at the same time, the vehicle of expression of overt Consciousness that has emerged and is self-aware in our physical energy-substance.
        Aurobindo, The Life Divine

14

Psychology and the New Physics

For every atom belonging to me as good belongs to you . . .

W. *Whitman*, Leaves of Grass

While weaving through the inner landscapes, the myriad fields of consciousness, the previous chapters have touched for periods on the great loom of physics. As a butterfly stops by each intricate flower, takes what it needs of sustenance, then flies off, we stop here and there in the shifting maze of modern physics, take what we need for nurturance and reference, then move on. We know that what we take is not the ultimate, but is grounding and necessary on our way.

In numerous ways this is a pivotal chapter. Earlier chapters have spoken of "fields" and "information," but have not fully explored their common root or origin. We hope to do that here. We have also talked about energy by way of analogy, but have not dealt explicitly with the energies of the material world in any real detail. We have stressed that the affective-ideational field of the Family Unconscious is vast and continuous in its interconnections. We hope to see how this same interconnectedness is an active reality on the material plane also. By so doing, we will make more clear the operation of the Family Unconscious in the material/energy world. Finally, we want to look briefly at the way matter, energy, and information or intelligence meet in a common ground. Springing from that ground, when properly nourished and comprehended, are the roots of transcendence.

At present there is a convergence of insights from modern physics and traditional views on the nature of consciousness as expressed in certain Eastern philosophical and introspective traditions. (1) This section will focus on four general areas as they relate to this convergence:

1. An emerging model or system that takes into account the new physics and also points up the limits of the older physical models of the psyche and the universe. This will lead to an outline of a hopefully more heuristic model. The new model will offer a greater integration of data from modern physics and traditional perspectives and will also incorporate the new psi data outlined in previous chapters.

2. The nature of perception and the ego's intimate involvement in this process. This will involve the functional use of ego and the ways in which the process of the ego is bypassed or transcended, not only in sleep but while we are wide awake.

3. The nature of consciousness emerging from the above formulations, leading to a new perspective on the ordering or levels of consciousness, as revealed by research data and introspective philosophical traditions.

4. An examination of how these data and new developments throw light on the traditional and the modern view of the Self.

With these four streams pouring into a common sea, we will be able to establish the mental and energetic aspects of the Family Unconscious firmly in the emerging paradigm that sees all this as an undivided whole. In exploring these converging areas it will be necessary to draw in some detail from physics, psychology, and new developments in neurology to support this emerging perspective which has been hinted at throughout this book.

Modern Western psychology has often based its

philosophical assumptions on models in current usage in physics. This is because physics and mathematics are often taken to be the most advanced of the basic sciences. Thus the Freudian psychology that emerged at the beginning of the twentieth century based a number of its philosophical assumptions and dynamic energy perspectives on the mechanistic model that dominated Western philosophical thought at that time. Behavioral psychology also based its paradigm on a mechanistic understanding of the laws of physics. Later Gestalt psychology and other more "humanistic" psychologies modeled their process along the organic or organismic lines. Each of these was an advance, but these developments were limited at a certain point, limited by dependence on the latest discoveries in the material world. Such discoveries and their resultant perspectives will always be supplanted later by new data in more heuristic models. This is also the case with the discoveries in modern physics. As such, data from the material "sciences" must always be held as "spiraling approximations" toward the truth but never directly reflecting any kind of ultimate truth. For now, we will present a viable way of knowing.

We approach the situation with what is currently known in modern physics about the most basic laws governing the material universe. Modern physicists presently enumerate four distinct kinds of interaction or forces to define the physical phenomena of the universe. These phenomena range from the astronomical to the subatomic level. These interactions or forces are as follows: 1) The *gravitational* interaction between particles and objects, more evident on an astronomical level. 2) *Electromagnetic* interactions of electrons and atomic nuclei, which are responsible for the more familiar physical and chemical properties of gases, liquids, and solids. 3) What are termed "*strong interactions*," which hold protons and neutrons together in the atomic nucleus. These strong forces act only within the inconceivably small range of about 10^{-13} centimeters, a distance which is insignificant in ordinary life. 4) What are termed *weak interactions.* They, too, are of unimaginably short range, 10^{-15} centimeters, and are not perceived as powerful enough to hold together any particular particles. They manifest only in certain collisions or decay processes that are not mediated by the strong or electromagnetic or gravitational forces.

While this most recent schema of forces and fields has a certain unitary sense about it, there are serious problems which the current theories have so far failed to solve successfully. Relativity and quantum mechanics, the two great pillars of contemporary physics, have led to a mathematical formalism termed quantum-field theory. In quantum-field theory all elementary particle interactions which create those fields of energy are "explained" on the basis of even more exchanges of elementary particles at "lower levels" of physical manifestation. In other words, the particles or bits of atomic and subatomic matter are seen as composed of even smaller bits of matter and energy.

Strangely, different kinds of particles in quantum-field theory are seen to turn into one another. The word *particle* in this context has come to convey, not a fixed material bit with definite boundaries, but something more like a dynamic interacting pattern of light.

The material/energy universe seems to be largely the product of these interacting fields of energy or light that take on different shifting identities. These different identities are what we know as matter. When free, all move at the speed of light, but they become trapped in different apparent forms, again creating what we call "matter." These so-called fundamental particles are indeed aspects of light, light which may actually, we believe, be the ground of their mutating identities. This means the present quantum-field theory approach is here somewhat extended to further seek the roots of interconnectedness. In other words, particles begin to appear as projections of the primary or "generalized light" energy, and particle exchange within this context occurs continually. They emerge from and return to the "generalized light" energy, which is paradoxically also the void.

Perhaps because of quantum-field theory, there has been a proliferation of elementary particles (neutrinos, pions, muons, etc.,) classified into families, leptons (massless or low mass particles) and hadrons (heavier mass and partaking in strong interactions). To get an idea of the relative "coupling strength" or power level of these four interactions, we can make the strong interaction equal to 1.0. Then the electromagnetic interaction would be 10^{-2}, the weak interaction is 10^{-5}, and the gravitational interaction would be 6×10^{-39}. Mostly these particles have a very short life-time, 10^{-20} seconds, but sometimes a little longer. (See appendix B.)

In particular we notice that through our present-day instruments and perception we see the strong force of the nuclear city to be the product of the continual exchange of particles called mesons by way of meson resonance of virtual particles. In other words, the exchange between particles which manifests as a field is accomplished by a transitional particle that occurs in the union of two mesons. These transitional particles (pi-meson, K-meson, Rho-meson, etc.) combine or lock together briefly (10^{-24} seconds), then separate. This is an aspect of the cosmic dance. It's as though they continually manifest different identities as they interact with each other. "Boundary" takes on a new meaning and an expanded flexibility in the overall play of reality.

Odder still is the fact that some of these particles (the proton and pi-meson) emerge from an uncharged particle (lambda), which itself seems to appear from cosmic debris and nothingness in the cloud chamber apparatus! (2) A very "strange particle" indeed. By appearing to come to our instruments out of nowhere, it appears nonsensical to us. Yet, if we had some wider field of perception or experience, we might be able to observe the "particle" in all its modifications and know its true nature. Its nature may well depend inextricably upon the nature of all other material/energy events.

It should be noted that all these forces or fields are *perceived* by us and by our measuring instruments as occurring *between* fields and particles. This leaves open the problem of what occurs when the distance decreases between these particle families and their constituents, termed quarks and leptons. In that realm the three known forces of subatomic interactions begin to blur, opening up the possibility of a single unified force of which the others are manifestations. This again brings up the idea of a primary or ground light of which the various particles and waves are projections. It is interesting that the weakest of the four forces or interactions, the gravitational force, is also the one we experience easily in our surface experience. This force that holds the stars and planets in orbit can be felt when we stand or walk. In a sense it stretches across a wide continuum and in a real way holds or enfolds all our material/energy experience.

The model based on these particles and their interactions shows a certain unitary quality. However there are at least five crucial problems for this paradigm. These five areas include the paradoxical identity of light; the "indivisibility" of the quantum domain; the shifting boundary and measurement problem embedded in the Indeterminancy Principle; the subtle subquantum dimensions where probability becomes problematic; and the apparent disjunction between continuous fields and discrete quanta, which may put quantum mechanics and Relativity on a collision course. It is important for us to have some idea of these problems in order to lay a foundation for the material/energy aspect of the Family Unconscious.

PROBLEMS AND HOLES IN THE FABRIC

The first problem concerns the understanding and perception of "light." This particular problem has led to some difficulties on the subatomic level. The perception of the phenomenon of light as a particle at times and a wave at other times has still not been fully resolved. For example, we know that light behaves as a wave in refraction and interference effects experiments where the number of quanta or energy bits is rather high. But light behaves as a discrete particle in other experiments such as the photo-electric current effect and the Compton effect of scattered X-rays, when low "numbers of quanta" are involved. Over a large number of particles or waves, the wave nature is seen; over small numbers, the particle nature is seen. In general, we can say that light behaves experimentally like a wave as long as no absorption or emission occurs, but when light is absorbed or emitted (as Blackbody radiation, etc.) the quantum or particle nature is observed. Note that we are "observing" through instruments we interpret on an explicate or explicit physical level.

The so-called "Copenhagen Solution" to this paradox by Bohr and his associates has so far held sway with the majority of physicists, but not all, as we shall see. This is the principle of complementarity, which holds that the wave function, the field characteristics of microphysics, describes an envelope over the statistical perturbations of particles. It is held here that particles and fields are complementary views of the same sets of occurrences. The Schrödinger wave-function equation describes this back and forth "behavior" of light acting as both particle and wave, but *also* introduces a universe of many other possibilities for each wave/particle. (3)

At the present time, therefore, we appear to settle for something like the following formulation. The nature of light depends on our measuring instruments; through some instruments it will appear as a particle and through others as a wave. It has a specific particle aspect, but also a dynamic pattern aspect. Perhaps it presents both these aspects to our instruments as it unfolds from a deeper order. This is true for the entire range of the electromagnetic spectrum, including X-rays, radio waves, microwaves, etc., not only for the limited visual range of 380 to 780 millimicrons. We are surrounded and infused by this particle/wave sea. The wave nature of light is crucial to our later discussion of mind, memory, and perception.

The second major difficulty is the fact that in the quantum domain the procedure by which we analyze classical systems into interacting parts tends to break down. This is evidenced when two entities combine to form a single system, such as in some of the above-mentioned elementary particle interactions. The process by which these separate entities combine cannot itself be split up into definite separate divisions. (4) In other words, there is a certain inherent indivisibility of quantum mechanical processes. We are confronted with the breakdown of our *perception* and ideas about the indefinite analyzability of each entity and process into various parts located in definite regions of space and time. Only when there are many quanta involved, such as on the everyday classical physical level, can such analysis be done with any real meaning. As a result of this insight, it is also only in the classical domain that we have a fairly recognizable concept of "matter" itself. Quantum theory has fatally wounded the mechanistic paradigm. The nineteenth-century dualism of matter and force has become suspect in recent physics. Each field of force is seen to possess energy and therein constitutes matter. Also each quantum field of force is associated with specific particles.

Thirdly, it is to be noted that since Heisenberg's Indeterminancy Principle we have been aware that our devices of measurement interact with what we are measuring and thereby change the process that we seek to measure. We, ourselves, are intimately involved in the process we seek to measure and know. This extends to the position and speed of a particle such that as we know more about one, we are required to know less about the other. We have only statistical norms to work with; no specifics or individual measurement is possible at this level. This interference with measurement has within it an implicit assumption that interference represents the boundary between subject and object, between our inner consciousness and external reality. Neither Schrödinger nor Heisenberg, however, could quite accept this implication. (5)

It should be noted, that at least for Schrödinger the laws of physics were believed to be absolutely physical and statistical in nature. Yet we do not really know, for instance, if ordinary physical laws hold for extremely small time and space intervals, since we can only test in the realm of macroscopic masses, i.e., large numbers of atoms. Our observations are statistical and require *belief* in their absolute validity when applied to novel situations. In other words, inductive reasoning is not without limits.

To the objection that theoretical physics is far removed from issues of the consciousness factor, we have only to notice that human consciousness can register a series of two or three photons in a dark adaptation experiment. In such experiments the subject is presented, in a completely dark setting, with tiny amounts or low quanta of light. The subject then responds to this light when it is emitted from the experimental apparatus. Surprisingly, it has been found that our consciousness experiences "discrete" quanta. (6) It has been suggested that the subject/object boundary doesn't belong in this domain because the interference is always by way of instruments; the actual observer remains "passive." However, we note that no one "simply observes" a sophisticated bubble chamber or particle accelerator. The observer is accompanied by theories, assumptions, technical history, and world views. The act of perception in this context is *active* and structuring.

Let it be stated clearly that it is the collapse or the "reduction of the wave-packet" nature of light that opens the way to the involvement of matter with the conscious observer. With observation the "behavior" of the wave-packet becomes limited, limited because its probability of being elsewhere is cancelled. Yet we would not limit consciousness to only this one observation. Dependent on the particular *state* of consciousness, i.e., its level of awareness of interconnectedness, only one or potentially *many* observations simultaneously can be known to an observing consciousness, i.e., many-worlds and/or one world alone can be known.

In terms of the proliferation of these "elementary" particles that keep appearing, Heisenberg (1975) himself has questioned the "elementary" status of each new particle that is hailed as the final elementary particle. In the British journal *New Scientist* Heisenberg, one of the parents of quantum mechanics, states that "what is becoming clear is that simple particle hunting—naming the parts—isn't taking us any nearer the elusive goal of elementarity... what is really needed is a fundamental change of concepts; we will have to abandon the philosophy of Democritus and the concept of fundamental elementary particles." (7) This brings us back to "undivided wholeness" and "interconnectedness." Interconnectedness would appear to be a more powerful model or schema than the yearly designation of the latest particle as the ultimate stuff of physical reality. We have marched from chemicals to elements to atoms, then from atoms to electrons, protons, and neutrons; from these have come the families of mesons, hadrons, and leptons. The most recent products of this paradigm are quarks with "flavor" and "charms." Holding these together are supposed "gluons." These then may be mediated by "virtual gluons." (8) Even this quantum field theory approach, termed Gauge symmetry, recognizes that at a certain level (10^{-33} centimeters and 10^{-44} seconds) quantum fluctuations of space-time become crucial and the meaning of the space-time continuum itself comes into question. Therefore, perhaps this process of perpetual discovery of new elementary particles may have more to do with *how* we observe that *what* we observe. However, an interesting synthesis or perspective might be gained by considering consciousness as an aspect of "natural" reality. If this were done, a basic symmetry might emerge in our experience and a kind of interconnectedness come into view. We would then begin to perceive these particles and their fleeting identities as localizations of energy unfolded from a more primary sea of light or energy.*

---

*This primary sea of energy, of which particle and wave are projections or abstractions, would appear virtually *limitless* as compared to the rest of material reality, and also paradoxically a void or emptiness. D. Bohm calculates that there is more such energy in one cubic centimeter of empty space at this "zero-point" of

The fourth problem with the model based on particles and their interactions occurs within shorter periods and distances, (10^{-33} centimeters and 10^{-44} seconds). At these levels, the statistical average field itself outlined by Heisenberg's principle of indeterminancy also appears to come into question. This subquantum level may be random as implied by quantum field theory, or perhaps is subject to lawful but hidden variables. (9) The definitive data are not yet in. However, it is quite possible that here at the sub-quantum mechanical level where space-time fluctuates, there are self-determining processes of the particles or fields, and these may well be relatively free of the restriction of statistical field approximations evidenced in "higher" level quantum processes. "Self-determined" implies a world with "self laws" inherent within the nature of the process itself. A non-field theory approach (such as the bootstrap theory of particle interaction) also stresses "self-consistency laws" of particle behavior at certain levels of material manifestation. (10) Without plunging into the intricacies of s-matrix theory (11) we can see how different models are leading to similar conclusions.

Finally on examining these anomalies in modern physics we are forced to note the potential inconsistencies between the internal structure of quantum and relativistic theories. The "excitation" of energy in a field is taken to be *continuous* in a relativistic framework; indeed, fields are continually expanding, colliding, etc. In the quantum field, on the other hand, the "excitation" of the field is perceived as discontinuous or *discrete* in quanta. The inconsistency arises at the subquantum level because "even in the 'vacuum' the field is so highly excited that the mean field in each region, however small, fluctuates significantly, with a kind of turbulent motion that leads to a high degree

---

energy than in the whole known material universe (Bohm, *Causality and Chance in Modern Physics*, 1957, p. 163-164.) Another reference to this manifest reality against a vaster unmanifest reality is found in the Vijnananauka Upanisahd where it is stated that "a particle of Its bliss supplies the bliss of the whole universe, everything becomes enlightened in Its light."

of randomness in the fluctuations. This excitation guarantees the discontinuity of the fields in the smallest regions." (12) The usual nonlinear equations are not sufficient for this fluctuating field. Other modes of "interconnection" are needed to deal with such phenomena. This requires a whole new principle.

SUMMARY

We have looked at the four presently known fundamental interactions or forces in the material world: the strong force or interaction of the atomic nucleus, the more noticeable electromagnetic force of everyday life, the ubiquitous gravitational force holding stars and planets in orbit in addition to keeping our feet on the ground, and the weak interaction or force, seen only in certain decay processes of the nucleus. These were seen to underlie all the interactions of the material world in one permutation or another. Yet as we looked closer, certain problems arose in the quantum relativistic paradigm that presently seems to explain all these interactions on the basis of even more subtle exchanges or interactions. These were the mutating identities of particles; the seemingly paradoxical behavior of light as particle and then as wave; the difficulty and indeterminacy of measurement in certain situations; the impossibility of division in the quantum domain; the rise of self-organizing principles on the subquantum level; and the apparent disjuncture between continuous fields and discrete quanta which may produce a crisis between quantum mechanics and Relativity at certain regions of phenomena (very high energies and momenta). All these factors contributed to the natural search for a paradigm that would integrate these diverse situations. Hunting for the latest "ultimate particle" seemed more and more like a mirage. Heisenberg, Capra, Bohm and others questioned this fragmented collection of particle after particle. From this fragmentation, a search for wholeness emerged. This search for wholeness, which bears a striking similarity to certain Eastern perspectives and approaches, began to focus on "data" from the material world that reflect the undivided wholeness or interconnectedness of the system. The findings of Bell, extrapolations from de Broglie, and the calculations of Bohm substantiated this view of an intimate and infinitely interconnected universe of which consciousness is obviously a crucial aspect. It was only a small step to realize that consciousness also is an undivided whole, a vast "field" that interconnects all other forms and levels of consciousness. This prepared the ground for a new and yet ancient principle of wholeness. It is to the root of union of this energy and information, and therefore consciousness, that we now turn our focus.

15

Interconnections:
Information and Energy

All these separations and gaps shall be taken up and
hook'd and linked together.
                    W. *Whitman,* Leaves of Grass

Early on in this century a young physicist, Louis de Broglie, noticed that since matter and energy were interchangeable through $E = MC^2$, matter itself must have wave properties like those of light. De Broglie reasoned that if light waves could behave like a stream of particles (as Einstein had proposed), then perhaps particles such as electrons could also possess wave properties. Thus both matter and light have an apparent dual wave-particle nature. For this insight put in mathematical form de Broglie received a Nobel prize. However, his insight went further than this. He noticed that a particle, in this case an electron, had a new kind of quantum mechanical field around it, similar to but also different from other fields. The "field" did not function based on the intensity or pressure of the field on the particle, but rather acted by the information content which is able to carry information about the whole experimental situation. Thus the *meaning* of the experimental result and the actual *form* of the experimental situation could no longer be separated! They were a whole, an undivided unity, a single process. In other words, knowledge, meaning and information were seen as embedded in the field itself. Both information or intelligence and matter were *organized* within the same process. The equations derived from this perspective fit the known data well.

This recognition began to make it clear that all material and energy interactions were somehow interconnected by their shared field. Thus, the material/energy level was seen as one vast field regardless of its location in space. This is very important from the standpoint of energy and information in the Family Unconscious. We have proposed a similar dynamic for the family system of shared energy, information, and affect.

After de Broglie, others noticed similar patterns of information/field process. Einstein, Podolsky, and Rosen (1) noted in some interesting experiments that information between some particles appeared to be communicated at speeds faster than light. This, however, seemed to be at odds with Relativity theory, in which light speed is the absolute speed. Quantum mechanics and Relativity appeared to collide around the communication of information. From the perspective of psi and the Family Unconscious, information appears not to be bound by conventional space, time, and speed considerations. This is in keeping with the research on psi at a distance, as previously elaborated. This opened up the issue of nonlocality by Einstein et al, and even by de Broglie. Somehow a spreadout, continuous "field" contained and communicated information. The idea of a primal sea of light or "generalized light" and information in various modes of operation again surfaces.

Later explorations of this great field came to be known as the "quantum interconnectedness of distant systems." The radical paradox of Einstein, Podolsky, and Rosen had matured into this concept, which was formalized by John Bell. (2) Recently positive experimental results have shown interaction across the field to be almost instantaneous. Again, this field carries both information and energy in one unified process. Naturally, those aspects of the field that share a closer affinity interact more intensely and obviously. This is the case in the material/energy world as well as in the field of the Family Unconscious. Both these realms constitute an undivided whole; both are trans-temporal and trans-spatial.

This present grasp of the material universe was finally crystallized by Bohm and Hiley (3) who outlined the integration of systems and subsystems and suprasystems. Since consciousness is a "natural process," it too is part of this vast system. Physicists like Wheeler (4) have also demonstrated this quantum interconnectedness by reference to a superspace or quantum foam which, given the collapse of classical space and time, create "worm holes" such that all parts of the universe are connected to all other parts. One immediately thinks of the Akasha Tattva of the ancient yogic seers. Wheeler, it should be pointed out, does not make this connection.

In any event, each of these operational theories of the material/energy world demonstrates the interconnectedness of the field. This is true of the vast "field" of consciousness also. De Broglie showed that matter was not only wave-like, but had a field aspect in which information about the whole was contained. Einstein et al showed the paradox of information at a distance communicated faster than light. Bell demonstrated the quantum interconnection of distant systems and his work in this area has recently been confirmed. (5) Wheeler has outlined another perspective on interconnectedness issuing from Relativity theory and introduced a universe of worm-holes through which even other potentially faster-than-light particles, Tachyons, could move. (6) Finally, Bohm has outlined the root of union of both matter and mind in a universe of undivided wholeness. Thus the material/energy world is seen as a field continually involved with itself with no break in process. The field of the Family Unconscious is seen in a similar light, the field being one of shared energy, affect and ideation. Psi is no stranger here, nor is the biogravitational field and numerous other interactions previously discussed. It is a field that, like matter itself, has aspects which are trans-temporal and trans-spatial in their root manifestation.

Experimentally speaking, "quantum interconnectedness of distant systems" has an even more direct and dynamic bearing on the process of psi information exchange in the Family Unconscious. In Relativity theory a signal is required for information exchange, whereas this is not necessarily so from the perspective of interconnected quantum processes. Some sort of "field" or process that *subsumes* both these perspectives is required. Remember "light" is neither particle nor wave completely, yet partakes of both identities as it unfolds from a deeper order. Remember how the "thought-germs" of the Mahayana Buddhists from their *Alayavijnana* or store-consciousness are projected outward, and how dreams in the family system are projections of the family's emotional matrix. We are suggesting here that a deeper aspect of the Self of a family member "resonates" with the deeper Self of another family member as on the subquantum level where particles have no separate identity. This deeper Self is a shared Self on the most profound level. The exchange of information is accomplished by "transmissions" of signals reverberating on the dualistic ordinary level from that of ultimate unity. In other words, that aspect which appears to be separate requires exchange because of that very separateness. The psi episode occurs as a unity, it is an integrated whole encompassing both levels. The conscious, thought-like awareness of the psi process creates the dualistic perception. This explicate aspect or phenomenal reality falls under the relativistic dimension of things separate in space and time. Thus, information appears to go from "here" to "there." On the other hand, the implicate aspect is the higher-order enfolded unity of which the explicate thought-awareness of the information is a manifestation. Thus if we recognize that each family member carries the Family Unconscious implicit or enfolded within him or her, we can see that the psi episode goes from ultimate unity, the sea of light mentioned earlier, to differentiated energy and information transfer. We can see how events separated by apparent distances on the explicit level have a strong and direct interconnection with each other at the implicate, unitary level. This "field" is a field of *shared* affect, energy, information, imagery, and *consciousness*. Requirements of both ultimate interconnectedness and signal exchange are satisfied when the shared field is recognized to be consciousness itself. Therein lies the process of nonlocality in psi events.

We suggest that this principle of dynamic interconnectedness of the whole system is not limited to laboratory experiments with helium atoms, etc., (7) but extends to the whole universe, of which consciousness is certainly an aspect. The holistic view of systems incorporated by greater systems and systems composed of subsystems, all in contact with each other at numerous levels, appears to provide an operational solution to the problem of nonlocality in the psi episode. This problem itself highlights the apparent disjuncture between the separate *localizable* events of relativity and the unbroken wholeness or quantum interconnectedness of the deeper or enfolded order. Such is the dissolution of mechanistic science.

In any case the five previously mentioned areas of difficulty indicate some anomalies or difficulties with the relativistic-quantum paradigm at certain levels of physical manifestation. Our proposed solution provides a bridge in the domain of psi as it operates in the shared Family Unconscious. Our theories are our perceptions, and in this sense we are in need of a different perception of events to account for much unexplainable data. It may be, as Capra suggests, that in the present era we are grappling most with a problem in perception.

TOWARD AN OPERATIONAL MODEL OF UNDIVIDED WHOLENESS

At this point it would be profitable to present a heuristic model that would help organize these ideas and data. In essence this model would need to be applicable not only to the domain of physics but also to biology, and particularly to that area most intimately connected with our intellectual seat, the crucible of neurology and psychology, the brain. A schema that allows each part to be connected intimately to every other part and still retain some differences is provided by the holographic model. We have spoken of this fleetingly in past chapters and now will digest it fully. Its central feature, the concept that each part is reflected or implicated in every other part, is a primordial idea. Perhaps, like the concept of number itself, it is an archetypal intuition of the human mind.

Ancient Tantric philosophy sounds the note that "in everything there is all that is in everything else." This insight echoes through the thought of Hippocrates, Agrippa von Nettesheim, and even Paracelsus. As far back as 1714 in the West, Leibniz, one of the discoverers of integral and differential calculus, pointed out in his philosophy of "windowless monads" that everything in the universe reflects everything else. In the 1920s Whitehead (8) elaborated the ontological principle that everything in the universe implies every other part of the universe. It was not until the 1920s, however, that a mathematician named Gabor created an explicit mathematical model that could be used for heuristic purposes in providing a rational working model of this process. For this he earned a Nobel prize.

Out of this eventually came the hologram. The principles of the hologram have been worked out in detail. (9) They involve the use of coherent light created by the laser to record on sensitive film, not a two-dimensional photograph, but an actual interference pattern of light waves which gives a three-dimensional image. Strangely, it turns out that from only a small part of this pattern, one can reconstruct the entire pattern, though with less detail. The correct decoding signal will *unfold* the entire "reality" of the image that was *enfolded* into every small part of it.

A model based on the holograph could make clear how one family member's dream enfolds all the other relations in that family matrix, the Family Unconscious. This holographic principle has been greatly expanded by other researchers including Pribram and Bohm into what is termed the *holomovement* or *holoflux.*

In Bohm's model of the universe, the holographic image or picture in 3D is analogous to the space-time world of the senses, the realm of separate objects. But rather than being the primary reality, this image is the outcome of the moving pattern of light bouncing off the object photographed. The image we see would be what Bohm calls the "explicit order" or "unfolded order," the manifestation in time and space of a reality from another, deeper dimension. The pattern of light, though captured on the photographic plate, actually exists only as waves and frequencies. This pattern is the "implicate" or "enfolded" order from which the image derives.

An analogy is seen in a television image. The visual image from the camera at the studio must be translated into radio waves which transmit it to our homes. The pattern in radio waves by no means has a one-to-one correspondence with the visual image. Yet the visual image is enfolded or implicated in the radio waves. Our television sets then explicate or unfold the order of the image, again making it visible or manifest.

Objects and events in nature are carried not only by light but by electron beams, sound, and innumerable other ways. The *holomovement* or *holoflux* are Bohm's names for the totality of all these carriers of the implicate order. This is the unbroken, flowing, ever-changing movement of all frequencies, light, sound, electron beams, all fields, both known and yet to be discovered. Notice here that the wave nature of matter implies an implicate order. This is crucial to ideas we will present in the final chapters of this book. Bohm uses a poetic analogy to express the relation of the holomovement to the material world: as clouds are formed by movement of the wind, so matter may be seen as manifesting the holomovement to our senses.

All the different aspects of the holomovement are inseparable. We can abstract out the light aspect, for example, to create a visual image. But in the holomovement light is merged with electrons, sound, and many other frequencies. "The totality of movement or enfoldment and unfoldment [is] the holomovement . . . . What is is the *holomovement*, and everything is to be explained in terms of forms derived from this holomovement." (10) In this view we see the world as emerging from an undivided, flowing background of energy and complex frequencies which carries patterns for everything which manifests from it. The holomovement is much vaster than what is unfolded and manifest: ". . . this implicate order implies a reality immensely beyond what we call matter. Matter itself is merely a ripple in this background . . . and the ocean of energy is not primarily in space and time at all." (11)

Because of the earlier stated difficulties with the quantum-relativistic model at certain levels of phenomena, we are beginning to cautiously consider the holonomic model. The different perspective of this holonomic view offers us a way of better organizing our theoretical and practical knowledge of external and internal reality. It may help resolve some of the crucial problems of the quantum relativistic model. It leaves us with a "process" universe in which all separation into discrete objects and discrete perspectives is questionable. However, it is also quite clear that for scientific purposes and simple everyday life we need a way to organize the moment-to-moment influx of data. The holonomic view provides for "levels" of abstraction in this undivided wholeness.

This view promises to do for contemporary science and our vision of reality what the lens did for an earlier science in opening new areas of research. Undoubtedly, this model will eventually be incorporated and transcended by paradigms as yet unimagined. This is the life-course of all heuristic and "mental" concepts. For now, however, it indeed captures "the spirit of the times" and provides a vital operational vortex of insights and parallels in the worlds unfolding before and within us. We sense that it presages a great shift in our perspective.

This wholeness, we may point out, not only encompasses

physical reality but also psychic and psychological reality. Thus the role and function of the ego of necessity comes into play. The role of the ego is intimately involved in the process of perception and also the process of knowing or epistemology. For that reason we must return briefly to the process of the ego we began in the previous chapter.

SUMMARY

We saw that presently there is a remarkable convergence on the nature of consciousness between insights from modern physics and certain powerful introspective traditions. Swimming through the world of particle physics with the aid of quantum mechanics and Relativity theory, we became aware of certain problems in our perception. By looking at the particles and fields within the context of the four presently known fundamental interactions of the material world, we came to see that hunting new particle after new particle, following the changling through identity after identity as it collided with different changling particles, did not bring us any closer to the "ultimate particle" or building block of nature. More and more these particles, which became waves when the circumstances were right, began to appear as manifestations of a deeper order in which they, as particle and wave, were projections. This great primal sea or background of energy was the root of these unfolding, fleeting identities through space and time. The interconnectedness of reality loomed into perspective. The reality of both the material and "mental" field became trans-temporal and trans-spatial.

This interconnectedness has a long philosophical and experiental history and recently has been empirically substantiated. From de Broglie to Einstein, Rosen and Podolsky to Wheeler and Bohm, and finally Bell, this great principle has taken firm root in the empirical world. The material/energy world is interwoven on innumerable levels and enfolds all aspects of the field. The field is seen as continuous in information and energy, just as is the field of the Family Unconscious. The nature of that field also appears to be one of energy, information and a permutation of light. We view psi as operating by processes outlined earlier and extending to all levels of reality. Levels of interaction are seen through this whole process. These levels are not frozen in the world of particles and waves, but also operate within that intimate cell we call the ego. It is that process in the ego that we now approach.

16

Ego, Duality, and Perception

The world is filled with the forms of the priesthood of Narcissus, all of which reinforce the sensation of separate existence and the dilemma that the sense of separate existence requires.

Da Free John, Garbage and Goddess

Nothing like it has occurred in years. At 10:45 p.m. you go out to the back porch and watch a family of shooting stars flash through the peerless sky on a disintegrating path to earth. Their arrival had been loosely predicted in the newspapers for weeks. Now the long-awaited light show veins the sky, and you and your friends have much to talk about. Several hundred miles away, buried deep in the astrophysics observatory, a group of researchers watch the same event. They vigorously debate the time sequence and amount of energy "released" in the fall of nickel ore and iron searing through the stratosphere. Each member of the team is highly trained and each observes something slightly different according to his or her interest in metallurgy, chemistry, or the motion of objects. Across the sea in a tribal land, steeped in field grass and the smell of fresh water a farmer witnesses the same display. To him it is his fertility god in the "upperlands" smiling down on him. He "knows" this to be a message from the great all-encompassing spirit and experiences a certain, tangible communion. He now feels hopeful of the new year's crops.

148

In each case the witness observed what was before him, felt separated from it, yet on some level knew it touched his life in the most intimate of ways. This sense of separateness seems to fluctuate greatly from time to time. Its management is the great thorn or stepping stone in our lives. Let's look closer at this most intimate of acts, perception.

LEVELS OF INTERCONNECTION

It is possible for you, the reader of this book, to detect an "observing ego" in yourself, and also that which is being observed now, this page. Try it. It is the nature of ego to create duality (you and the page). However, if we are also confronted ultimately with a universe of "undivided wholeness in flowing movement," we need to examine the ego and its relationship to our perception of, and involvement with, this undivided wholeness. In other words, we need to consider the relationship between the unifying process and the ego's differentiating process. We are here sharply restricting the concept of "ego" to the sense of "I-ness." We will not deal with the complex executive functions of the ego, its shifting identification with external objects and requirements, and its various developmental stages as elaborated from Freud to Sullivan to Klein. The ego or sense of "I-ness" here is also seen as distinct from its accumulated memories (or *chittas* in Yogic terminology) and its sensorimotor demands (or *manas*).

Aurobindo outlines the function and the process of the ego in relationship to the primal unity of undivided wholeness in flowing movement:

> Our surface cognition, our limited and restricted mental way of looking at ourself, at our inner movements and at the world outside of us and its objects and happenings, is so constituted that it derives its different degrees from a fourfold order of knowledge. The original and fundamental way of knowing, native to the occult self in things, is a knowledge by identity; the second, derivative, is a knowledge by direct contact associated at its roots with a secret knowledge by identity or starting from it, but actually

separated from its source and therefore powerful but incomplete in its cognition; the third is a knowledge by separation from the object of observation, but still with a direct contact as its support or even a partial identity; the fourth is a completely separative knowledge which lies on the machinery of indirect contact, a knowledge by acquisition which is yet, without being conscious of it, a rendering or bringing up of the contents of a pre-existent inner awareness and knowledge. (1)

Thus we can see that there are "levels" of awareness and involvement with the primal reality of undivided wholeness. This first knowledge, knowledge by identity, involves a deep identification with or fusion or lack of separation from the object of perception. (Notice how in separation is rooted the notion of space.) In other words, this kind of knowledge is the awareness of undivided wholeness in flowing movement, or the indivisibility of the process at all levels (not only at the quantum level of perception). It is a knowledge that does not recognize separation between observer and what is observed. This occurs sometimes when one is swept away totally by an emotion, losing oneself in something beautiful, in another person, in the luminous ecstasy of nature, and in the mystical experience. Each one of us reading this can draw from the web of his or her life some fleeting, balanced moment when we felt at-one-ment with everything.

The second kind of knowledge is a knowledge by direct contact, which is at bottom based on a knowledge by identification and intuition of the subliminal mind. This may be that level of our being or psyche in which psi processes occur. Indeed, Aurobindo points out that "it is the subliminal in reality and not the outer mind that possesses the power of telepathy, clairvoyance, and second sight and other super-normal facilities whose occurrence in the surface consciousness (ego) is due to openings or lifts in the walls erected by the outer personality's unseeing labor of individualization interposed between itself and the inner domain of our being." (2) In modern Western psychology this might be the knowledge that is subliminal or at a pre-conscious/unconscious level in our perception. Needless to say, there is an awareness, but it is an awareness of a very dim level that does not reach waking consciousness. This is the level of shared consciousness.

Third in this process of separation from undivided whole-ness in flowing movement is a knowledge by separation from the object of observation. This still involves some partial knowledge by identification. It is that level of ego differentiation when the sense of differentiation itself over-powers the sense of identification. That name on the tip of your tongue for days that you can't seem to remember and the powerful dream that you can't quite grasp the meaning of are only two kinds of experiences from this level. Of necessity, these are obviously graduated degrees of ego-awareness. The self still cognizes its identity with the object but pushes to its extreme the play of intimate separateness. At first there is not a sense of Self, only of self and other self.

Finally there is completely separative knowledge. This separative knowledge is the functioning of the observing ego proper. This ego uses imagery and sensory data to construct a working theory of the external world. At the point of constructing and interpreting the world outside, it begins to identify with its theory and in the process assumes that the inner world is a direct reflection of that external world. In other words it begins to identify with what it ciphers and observes. It therein is seduced by phenomena.

In the Vedantic perception of things there is first of all pure awareness out of which the external data of the world is constructed as we intuit an external world. This is the direct experience of the world as undivided wholeness in flowing movement. The Kung Fu master at a certain stage in the student's development places him in a darkened room. Without sight the student learns the smell and subtle sound and feels the thermal vibration of his opponent. All this "data" is then integrated and acted upon by the student in the quiet, absolute dark.

Reflection on the part of the reader will indicate that the

incoming data is first organized by our sensorimotor apparatus and then interpreted by our intelligence and by our ego. Eventually we construct a theory of the external world based upon the data we receive from outside. However, that data is secondary to the pure immediate awareness within the psyche itself. In other words, our knowledge of the material world does not come from "immaculate perception" or "direct touch," but is inferred from our representations of it to ourselves.

These ways of knowing and perceiving point out that the ego, though necessary, leads inevitably to duality and as such is not equipped to reflect the undivided wholeness of the universe. Yet it originates and translates out of a knowledge by identification, which is the fundamental knowledge. Again Aurobindo:

> In the supreme timeless Existence, as far as we know it by reflection, Existence and consciousness are one. We are accustomed to identify consciousness with certain operations of mentality and sense and, where these are absent or quiescent, we speak of that state as being unconscious. But consciousness can exist where there are no overt operations, no signs revealing it, even where it is withdrawn from objects and absorbed in pure existence or involved in the appearance of non-existence. It is intrinsic in our being, self-existent, not abolished by quiescence, by inaction, by veiling or covering, by inert absorption or involution; it is there in the being, even when its state seems to be dreamless sleep or blind trance or an annulment of awareness or an absence. In the supreme timeless status the consciousness is one with being and immobile, it is not a separate reality, but simply and purely the self-awareness inherent in existence. (3)

In the holonomic or holographic paradigm, the ego can be identified with the explicate order, whereas the implicate order is much closer to knowledge by identification. Between the implicate knowledge by identification and the completely separative knowledge of the explicate order, there are derivative layers or levels of ego-bound consciousness and a deeper knowledge which corresponds to our subliminal psyche. Implicit in this is a sense of order in nature and order in consciousness itself.

The ego is not the problem, but rather the way we use it. Clearly we need an observing ego in our daily lives. The ego is a necessary and transitional phase in the evolution toward something else. It must be sufficiently developed in order to transcend itself, at times quiet enough to be translucent.

In summary, it appears as though the very nature of ego is to create duality, to divide the world into subject and object. This duality pervades all our daily-life perceptions as well as our science. It may indeed be that our perception of light from an ego perspective in itself gives us the wave/particle dilemma. In other words, it may be the psyche's apperception of the dualistic level that creates the present anomaly of the nature of light. Remember that in the province of the Indeterminacy Principle, when the problem of measurement arises the interference with measurement appears at the boundary between subject and object. It is the actual collapse of the wave-packet into only one perceived situation from a number of other possibilities that accounts for this. It is only by moving toward wholeness, focusing on transcending and thereby being able to operate outside of linear space and time categories, that we can escape this duality. Not only does light have a wave/particle nature, but also each particle seems to have an anti-particle. This is not a sterile academic point, but pervasive in a very intimate process.

In the Family Unconscious we are constantly dealing with shared realities of a most intimate nature in a situation where initially there may be little differentiation between psyches in the field. The shared dream image or motif, or even the actual psi event, highlights the fact that subsystems, localizations in the greater field that we might refer to as individual members, are incorporated into greater information systems or fields for the purpose of communication of significant information. The "boundary" is not always clear; the difference between subject and object is flexible. Attempts to objectively know and measure in this province will always have these problems embedded in them. In such states as dreaming, deepest sleep, psi, and some levels of meditation, interpenetration and intimate interconnectedness become foreground or the main field. This interpenetration of subjects, and the fact that matter or "objects" are wavelike in nature, throws light on another issue rampant in the Family Unconscious.

Since in reality "objects" are trapped light held in patterns, this means that all "objects" interpenetrate at some level. The introjected object of the "object-relations school" of ego psychology is really an integration of energy fields into the greater field of oneself. In other words, the emotionally powerful, formative person in our development, e.g., mother, uncle, is not merely an image we carry around, but a dynamic pattern of force that actively interacts with us. This is an affectively-energetically active aspect of another person. Said another way, no "object" is ever introjected, rather the energy/information pattern of the significant other is integrated into one's own system. The family system in which this dynamic pattern is not managed well produces various syndromes, especially the borderline patient. The back-and-forth movement of the psyche of the borderline personality between emotional isolation and the fear of drowning his or her identity in others in the search for real intimacy is a reflection of the psyche's unstable introjected Family Unconscious energy pattern around certain themes. The therapist sees this often, but it will elude his or her grasp unless the nature of the energy pattern, not introjected object, is assessed. In a real sense there are no individuals on the primary level; rather in this enfolding field there are degrees and levels of concentration. The great field is nonlocal in nature.

This process occurs in every family. However, only in certain kinds of family interaction does the borderline or "psychotic insight" pattern emerge. It is true that such patients do have more psi capacity than most, but it is transient and passes with the high crest of this disorder. The borderline personality moves back and forth between extremes of complete union and love and reactionary isolation and anger. Such a person must learn functional boundaries and learn to be permeable but stable. Being able to see compassion rather than death and anger makes the boundary experience reinforcing.

From our work with such people we have come to believe that the borderline patient and sometimes the psychotic have a tangible experience of undivided wholeness, of our interconnectedness, and what we have done with it. Briefly, they see past the illusion of individuality and know that there are no separate selves. This is terrifying to the mind that "sees" the world as separate, distinct, material, atomistic. It is the mouth of death. For a fleeting period they glimpse the ocean of interconnectedness, then become afraid they will drown.

We are not encouraging the development of such pathological states. Rather, we feel that such states are often the upsurge or breaking into consciousness through the pressure of life exigencies of energies of a new and authentic reality. But the person is not ready or trained to deal with this flood into his or her system. Each day we all play an intimate cosmic game with each other where you pretend not to be me and I accept your counterfeit signature.

Thus when the ego can consciously recognize its "resonate affinity" with certain significant others of its Family Unconscious system, then it can safely feel and see its own reality tangibly reflected in the other. The usual healthy reaction to this is compassion and a sense of intimate connection with all else. The capacity to observe is the great gift of the ego, but it can become a tomb of obsessional rumination as well as a tool for transcendence.

THE OBSERVING EGO AND THE WAVES OF THOUGHT

It is interesting to note that the ego itself can observe many of the processes of the psyche and consciousness.

This fact points out that ego and "thought" are not identical. It is true that the ego can identify itself with its thoughts and very often does so. But a prolonged reflection and meditation by the reader will show that we can be aware of thoughts from a perspective that is not quite "thought" itself. In other words, awareness itself is not always manifest as thought. An intermediate manifestation of this is noting that there is a difference between our language and what we thought. We are herein drawing a distinction between ego-awareness and the thoughts of the ego. These thoughts, including those of the reader at this very minute, can also be perceived and experienced as waves or energy.

Swami Rama, a fully realized master of Raja Yoga, demonstrated at Menninger Clinic his conscious control over not only alpha, theta and delta brainwaves, but also over a host of other behaviors previously thought to be involuntary. He speaks of the "thought-waves" of the mind. (4) Ajaya also points out that there are particular technologies and techniques for directing and controlling these various thought-waves. (5) Indeed, the whole science of yoga as codified by Patanjali is the science of controlling the "thought-waves" of the mind. Clearly, in order to control thought there must be an observer of thought other than thought itself. This is a difficult concept for Westerners. The best way to grasp it is to reflect quietly on your own thought processes. You will notice that briefly and periodically you are aware and can grasp the totality of the meaning of your thoughts from a position that is outside the linear progression of thoughts or stream of consciousness. It does not matter if instead of waves you experience bits or particles of thought. Both are projections of a deeper order and can be influenced. Some of this is no doubt rooted in our brain processes.

The ancient idea that thought presents itself in terms of "thought-waves" has some interesting new neurological experimental support. Karl Pribram, a neurosurgeon whose work we will look into in the next chapter, has been able to identify two classes of brain coding operations in the neural pathways. (6) One is the *discrete* impulse type seen in nerve discharges. The other is a *continuous* steady-state microstructure created on the neural junctions themselves. In this context, the discrete vs. continuous pattern is one of organized information and matter embedded in the neural substance and process itself.

In some Eastern and yogic traditions, thought is seen as a "living force," a position which has immense clinical and philosophical implications. (7) We have seen that there is thought as distinguished from an observer of thought. Is it also possible to have consciousness without thought, albeit very briefly? As one practices and deepens in meditation, there comes the experience of clear consciousness without an object of thought. It should be remembered at this point again that according to the theory of Relativity "objects" are really "events" in space-time. Interestingly enough, this view is also found in Mahayana Buddhism.

> The views of space and time which I wish to lay before you...
> are radical. Henceforth space by itself, and time by itself, are
> doomed to fade away into mere shadows, and only a kind of
> union of the two will preserve an independent reality
> (Minkowski, 8).
> We look around and perceive that... every object is related
> to every other object... not only spatially, but temporally....
> As a fact of pure experience, there is no space without
> time, no time without space; they are interpenetrating
> (Suzuki, 9).

The convergence of these two perspectives, one a Western scientific and the other an intensely introspective Eastern perspective, would indicate that consciousness is the ground out of which all objects and space-time events evolve and unfold. One can, of course, speculate that one is having thoughts and that one understands those thoughts by other thoughts, and that one understands one's understanding thoughts from a perspective of more thoughts, ad infinitum on down to an infinite regress. However, an intuition will point out that at some point one understands thoughts from a perspective that is outside of thought. A mathematical parallel to this problem is seen in Von Neumann's "catastrophe of infinite regression," the solution of which draws consciousness inexorably into the physical universe as an agent or "hidden variable." Western perspectives are beginning to confirm the ancient Eastern insight that consciousness is primary, the undivided ground of wholeness behind our familiar space-time world of discrete objects and persons.

17

Neurology and Consciousness

*... ephaptic and synaptic events, those that are com-
posed at the junctions between neurons, form a pattern
... these patterns make up wave fronts.*
K. Pribram, Languages of the Brain

THE CORTICAL FIELD: PLAYGROUND OF
LIGHT AND INFORMATION

The opening moments of Beethoven's Ninth Symphony are
high, thin, and clear. We are suspended in space and in-
different to time. Quietly energy, sound, and meaning
unfold from a seed idea, until the creation extends out wave
after wave, ending in an explosion of patterns which outline
the future course of the event. As much power and effect
lie in the pauses between notes as in the melody and
rhythms that interconnect them. Wave upon wave of this
elemental music spreads through our entire body/mind
network.

The brain, of course, is involved in an experience like this.
There is considerable experimental evidence that wave
patterns, once initiated, spread over large areas of the
brain, forming synchronized oscillations or vibrations of
energy that reflect each other. (1) This becomes clear in
the work of Eccles in neurology. Furthermore, once we
have really heard or learned the wave patterns of
Beethoven's Ninth or other wave patterns, the memory
is not located in one place but somehow retained by us in

many different brain structures simultaneously, that is to say, in a nonlocal way. (2) Perhaps this is partially what is meant when someone tells us that he or she "feels" the music deep in his bones and nerves. Therefore, in a world where waves with information are constantly being synchronized over time and interfaced, as occurs in the system of the Family Unconscious, the influence of wave patterns becomes immense.

It seems that neurologists have produced a good deal of data that suggests that the "aware" aspects of consciousness present themselves to us in wave-like manners. We said earlier that the wave-like or field character of light is an extremely important aspect of our direct experience. Here we are drawing heavily from the work of Nobel prize-winning neurologist Sir John Eccles.

Actually Eccles was influenced in this area of wave-pattern observation by Sherrington, who in turn influenced Lashley, who in turn touched Pribram. (3) In any event, Eccles extended the initial work that indicated that there were innumerable interconnections within the neurological network of the brain. The synapses are points at which nervous impulses pass from one nerve cell to another. They were shown to be highly active specialized junctions where the brain cell membranes are extremely close to each other, transmitting signals from one cell to the next in many directions. The distance between brain cells (only 180 to 200 angstrom units across) is small enough for quantum processes conceivably to operate. A neuron has the power of about one thousand-millionth of a watt. In fact, the whole process of the brain requires very little to operate on, roughly 10 watts for the human brain. It is obviously extraordinarily sensitive to electrical stimulation and reception. Some children, using biofeedback instruments, have been able to use the electrical energy of their own brain to power small train sets.

An impulse is relayed across a synapse in an "all-or-nothing" manner. It has an electrical effect of .001 volts and lasts .01 to .02 seconds. It then requires about 10 times this much voltage to reach a critical level such that the neuron will discharge again. This sequence of rising electrical charge with eventual discharge and then re-fractoriness with resistance to stimulus, followed again by rise, is seen as a rhythm of the brain wave. We spoke of these brain waves in our chapter on sleep.

There are numerous such events in the brain acting upon each other at any given time. Stimuli from the external world through sense organs are carried by electrical charge through the neural pathways to the various areas of the brain. This subtle electrical stimulation is occurring all the time. A pulse or propagation is created by this traffic, the many cells activated in parallel at each synaptic linkage in this chain. In fact, these events acting upon each other in-volve crossing over each other and emerging at different points in the brain. These multiple wave fronts propagating at the same time lead to the pooling ᴜf waves and give an onward propagating wave sharing the summation or com-bined cha.acteristics of other waves. The wave frᴜnt area therein can involve surrounding areas of the brain's network.

A small, initial cortical stimulation of only 100 neurons at a relay stage can develop quickly into a propagating wave moving across the brain involving nearly 100,0ᴜ0 neurons a second. These waves "reverberate" through the synapses with "external stimuli" and are also "self-reexciting." Therefore to a certain extent they are stable events in time as they do not depend entirely on shifting sensory input. This is an important finding because of its implica-tions for the way our memory of things remains stable.

It is essential to note here in this simplified presentation of a rather complex process that brain cells in the cortex operate not only on the surrounding areas in the neural network (through short branches from their axons) but also upon cells and synapses in remote parts of the network. The cells in one hemisphere of the brain can activate the symmetrical region of the other hemisphere (through the ridge of the corpus callosum that interconnects both

hemispheres with specialized nerve pathways). The interaction of these various wave fronts issuing from various
specific sites in the cortex affect the integration and synthesis of the information relayed through the neural
network.

The wave characteristic or some other recognition factor
of the wave front must be kept in some form or other for
this integration process to occur. Thus the process is seen
by Eccles and others as an ordered pattern of curving, loop-
ing wave fronts acting through millions of neurons, creating
layers and patterns of currents from millisecond to millisecond. This activity is a subjective counterpart to one level
of awareness. In particularly "creative moments," we
develop wave patterns in the brain due to concentration on
a creative problem. These patterns then "emerge and
transcend" the existent patterns to form a more "resonant-
like intensification" of activity in the cortex, which brings
a new pattern to conscious attention.

We note that the brain's neurological system provides
data to an observer or integrater of this material, who then
takes the data and interprets external reality. This again is
the Vedantic position. This would seem to parallel the
process of some point of pure awareness within us intuiting,
interpreting, and labeling the external sensory and motor
world into an intelligible pattern. This "still point of the
turning world" is the witness, the observer.

The above-mentioned creative interludes require
previous use of patterns in the synaptic knobs, those cups at
the end of nerves that touch and greet each other. This
previous use of such patterns and imagery is generally
termed memory. Pribram has focused a great deal of attention on the process of memory and has discovered what
changes occur at the synaptic knobs that seem to account
for memory storage. After noting the specific areas of visual,
auditory, somesthetic or sensory and motoric areas in the
cerebral cortex, he notes that very often injury to these
areas does not significantly disrupt memory function. He
points out that surgical removal of up to 95% of a cat's

optical tract, as done by Galambos at the University of California in San Diego, did not significantly affect the animal's ability to perform highly complex visual tasks. Mica strips and even aluminum hydroxide cream in the cortex of some animals didn't severely impair their pattern recognition. This suggested that memory storage was completed by information being distributed to many parts of the system in a more or less nonlocal way. This made the memory material in both humans and non-humans (monkeys and cats) retrievable, even though the specific regional site of the material may be injured in some way. (4, 5) The storage of memory by this holographic analogy has received independent support by Campbell (6), Pollen (7), and others. This research has focused on the visual system but may be extended to all sensorimotor systems.

From Eccles' work we see that the unfolding waves of Beethoven's Ninth Symphony create sensory data that enter the brain from the specific sensory organs by a sequence of electrical wave-front patterns. Pribram has shown that these wave fronts are encoded and distributed over wide regions of the cortex. This distribution and storage resemble the functioning of the hologram as outlined earlier. This change and integration of the wave fronts appears to parallel the Fourier transformation in which a wave pattern can be generated by a specific set of frequencies. (According to Fourier's theorem, any smooth periodic function may be represented as the sum of a number of sinusoidal waves with frequencies that are multiples of one basic frequency.) Similarly, the interference pattern or interconnecting waves that produce a hologram have a unique capacity to be reconstructed from only a part of the pattern, since that part has implicit or enfolded in it all the other parts. (In other words, each part contains implicit within it every other part.) This is the structure of a holonomic paradigm and demonstrates "neatness of fit" to these new findings about the brain. These transformations are actually coding actions. Pribram describes how the aggregate of slow potentials in the wave fronts generated in the brain over time and location at any moment creates a state which has a microstructure that provides a basis for memory. (8) The microstructure itself is the neural junction which can become part of an organization and temporarily unrelated to the receptive field of any particular neuron. It is a neural state that is acted upon and can act on arriving nerve impulses.

The frontal cerebral cortex or front part of the brain is of paramount importance in man and primates for these processes. Pribram has indicated that the neural network has literally millions of interference patterns resulting from the transformations generated by wave fronts from the synaptic processes. The neural network would appear to be characterized by a highly complex pattern of *light* and *vibration* through time. These transformations generate a microstructure of synaptic events that, regarded as wave fronts, set up interference patterns with other wave fronts leading to a holographic structure. Again this is occurring at the synaptic junctures. As such, since these are executed in the frequency domain, it is the matrix of neural potential (waves that are continuous) not the nerve impulses (all-or-none discrete firing) that is implicated.

The cells in the brain are tuned to specific *resonant* frequencies, a process which allows these frequencies to be recognized, i.e., remembered when the correct Fourier transform code is given. Thus many different patterns can be stored in the same area, since it is a matter of frequencies and not of space that is involved. This allows the holographic model to have "content addressability" as opposed to spatial or "location addressability," a principle on which many computers now operate. This is closer to our model of the unconscious which is a non-spatial model.

We should note that these images, wave fronts, and memory processes are perceived by an "observer" who is not just another image. We have seen that this is no problem from the yogic and Vedantic perspective. However, Pribram attempts to explain this by making the neural processes isomorphic to or a reflection of physical reality and thus making the observer and the observed one. This "sensorimotor reciprocity theorem," it seems to us, limits the range of the "data" that can be received and coded by the Fourier transform to the motor schemas of the organism. This precludes the organism's awareness of more "subtle" energies in the environment and in its own subtle structure. Also the Schrödinger wave function equation, which as we have seen opens the door to numerous other universes for each particle/wave, is not admitted into the scheme. We are restricted to the immediate physical universe of the senses, which can be trained to ignore equally viable realities. However, the perception of the cerebral cortex as a highly complex shifting sea of patterns leading to stabilized holographic events is an extraordinarily powerful heuristic paradigm.

In terms of thought processes, we do not wish to leave the impression that thoughts are "electrical." Rather we as a biosystem use the electromagnetic energy level for various purposes. More subtle energies at the level of the quantum domain are also utilized by a focused consciousness. Our experience of our thoughts is the subjective side of these neurological events.

The Greater Field and the Family Unconscious

In an interesting paper by Walker (9) there is outlined in exquisite detail a mathematical and biochemical model for energy transfer at the synaptic level. The processes here can be seen to reflect the processes of consciousness at the quantum and subquantum levels. Eccles was first to introduce the wave front as a model for thought and consciousness and its operation in the brain. Pribram elucidated how this process of memory and wave front is stored at the synaptic junctions by the interference patterns, resulting in a stable hologram decodifiable by a Fourier transform. Walker has calculated the exact energy transfers involved at this level. At the synaptic junctions, which again are roughly 180 to 200 angstroms apart, it requires only .070 eV (i.e., electronvolts) in mammals to affect the potential

energy of a single electron in the membrane field implicated in consciousness. Thus the energy required to transmit "information" across synapses is indeed extremely
small. It requires very little bioenergy to affect behavior
at the quantum level of functioning. One is reminded of
the biogravitational field of Dubrov and associates that we
examined in Section Two.

This synaptic transfer that leads to the energy exchange
as described by Walker is accomplished by a transfer of
electrons between molecules through a quantum mechanical tunneling effect. In this subtle process very weak
currents are involved as one large or macromolecule exchanges an electron with another macromolecule and a
certain amount of energy is "released." There is a certain
affinity here to the weak interaction of the four basic interactions or forces in nature we discussed earlier, especially the weak force shown in the decay process of the
nucleus. This transfer involves an electron going from one
quantum level to another, often to a higher energy level.
This produces a conformational or structural change in the
macromolecules themselves. With continual usage an open
but stable system is produced which could provide, again, a
global storage for memory. Remember, an electron has a
particle and wave aspect. Walker does not directly employ
the holographic model but does speak of the same energy
process which occurs in synaptic and ephaptic junctures.
Psi for him does not involve "energy" transfer for information transfer. See our discussion of this in the chapter on
Information and Energy.

At this juncture it is helpful to quote directly from
Dubrov's research on the biogravitational field which
appears to "arise in consequence of changes in the conformation of protein structures as a result of the transformations which occur with polypeptide molecules. These
changes in conformation induce a strictly ordered,
structural crystalline state of the hydrated protein molecules, and their *oscillations are synchronized* [italics mine],
as a result of which a qualitatively new physical situation is

established, affecting the atom's symmetry groups and the nature of the sub-molecular space." (10) In other words, this biogravitational field appears to interact at the quantum level with some sort of mechanical tunneling effect or even more subtle "worm hole," making possible the psi transmission. A greater emphasis on how psi events affect the physical world outside the body, especially those events on the quantum level, can be seen in experiments in metal-bending, magnetization, and other psychokinetic events which Hasted (11) and other experimental physicists have measured under the most stringent conditions.

In terms of the Family Unconscious, we note simply that families, in addition to their genetic similarities and their recurrent transactional patterns over years and sometimes generations, also sleep and unconsciously process data together. Year after year after year of sleeping in the same house, family members bring into play the coordinating processes elaborated throughout this book. These are resonate affinities between them and within each of them. At a certain level, remember, both the worlds of matter and of mentation go trans-spatial and trans-temporal. "Below" the level of imagery associated with commerce at the synaptic junctures that Pribram reveals, there is still activity of a sort. We believe that there are still deeper symmetries in matter and energy and consciousness that are self-organized. These oscillations in matter and energy are coordinated with oscillations throughout the greater field of which the person is a part. This greater field includes the energy centers or plexuses (chakras) implicated in psi. A certain "order" is coordinated by an information field that is nonlocal in nature and yet highly articulate. This again is an aspect of psi in the Family Unconscious.

SUMMARY AND INTIMATIONS

We have followed the initial sensations from wave front to Fourier transformation frequency to encoded synaptic hologram and memory storage. This process involves wave front transformations which are subjectively experienced in the stable process as memory. Still open, however, is the issue of who or what *has* the memory, where the observer is in this process. How does the observer choose between the many worlds possible on the sensory, cognitive, and even quantum mechanical level?

This memory bank is referred to as *chitta* in yoga psychology. It is seen as separate, not only from the observing "I" or ego, but also from the sensory focus areas themselves, e.g., hearing, touch, smell, sight, and taste. These sensory specific cortical receiving sites receive specific neuro-electric activity patterns from the organism. (12) These patterns are not only muscle movements, etc., but complex action patterns that can be applied by the cortex to novel situations. These sensory functions are termed *manas* in yogic literature and belong to the sensorimotor aspect of the psyche. Through specific techniques the ego and eventually the deeper "Self" can acquire the power to control these thought waves and memory processes.

It strikes us that these wave fronts, which are obviously observed and may potentially be controlled by the inner observer, are actually vibrations of the organizational structure of the brain and psyche. In other words, these waves are a permutation of energy or light. The sine waves of all these wave fronts are coded in a process seemingly identical to the Fourier transform, and yet there remains the perspective that is "aware" or witnesses these waves. Some of these waves are experienced as thought patterns. Since these waves occur in space and time and are explicit, the observer of these waves, by virtue of being able to observe, ultimately is not in space and time but rather outside them and of the implicate order. Space and time may well be intuitions or categories of the mind learned and structured developmentally in childhood, not the ground of the mind itself.

The ego in the holoflux or holonomic sea is explicit and therefore separated from the object of perception. Our earlier analysis of the ego has shown that this function of the Self not only creates the perception of separate and discrete "objects" but is also a process of emergence from the implicate order. Remember that from relativity theory and also from Mahayana Buddhist introspection we know that as "objects" we exist as "events" in space-time. We also know that, divorced from the *manas* of perception and the memory bank of *chitta*, we are pure awareness and as such are the source or the ground out of which space and time are constructed. Space and time appear to be ultimately intuitions of the Self.

This Self or observer is therefore not the ego that is locked in space and time. The ego goes through many *modifications* and disappears in sleep. However, the reader will note that occasionally he or she is "aware" during sleep. This awareness is usually reflected through REM dream states, as seen in the chapter on sleep. If one is awakened during sleep but not in REM, one has fragmentary remembrances of ideation. We also know, however, from the technique of Yoga Nidra and lucid dreaming that one can develop an awareness of REM dream states and other non-dreaming states that occur during sleep. This practice of Yoga Nidra again involves going deeply into the delta and sometimes low theta EEG state that is usually correlated with deep dreamless sleep. An ancient psychological text, the *Taittiriya Upanishad*, locates this deepest Self outside the mental constructs of space and time and beyond the wave fronts or *chitta* of memory and the sensory demands or *manas* of the external worlds. This awareness is always there but may be only subliminal when we are in the waking state. Where is this Self, however, in the scheme of the holoflux that we have been exploring?

18

The Self and Perception

That wherein disappears the whole of that which affects the mind, and that which is also the background of All; to THAT I bow, the all eternal consciousness, the witness of all exhibitions of the Intellect.
Upadesasahasri Upanishad

Thanksgiving is perfect this year. Sitting to your right at the table your favorite aunt smiles, passes you the dish you usually take a little too much of, and makes some remark about how good she feels. It's directed to you but clearly reflects the atmosphere of everyone at dinner. Laughing, you agree and casually look away. Not particularly focused on anyone, satiated, relaxed, you quietly notice how suffused with peace and balance you feel. Above your brother's head, caught in an antique frame on the wall, is a photograph of a deceased relative you've shared many such times with, and you feel even more deeply at peace and sense the community beyond the present context.

Without much reflection, you quietly feel all your relationships alive in you, both from the past and now. Each one has influenced your life in innumerable ways. Things feel immediate, affectively strong and calm. Many barely articulated memories drift through your mind. Quite easily you see your own mannerisms and habits and other aspects of yourself appearing slightly differently in each person, in each relationship. You can even feel the relationships between others as they must at least partially feel these. You realize this whole feast/ceremony of cycling food and nourishment with the family is older than you. Without effort you sense what such a group would have looked and felt like many years ago. A little expansion sees the same story in different times, different ages. You even see such a celebration slip beyond cultural and racial boundaries as it arches back across history to some preliterate gathering around an ancient, ancestral fire. All this passes in a wordless instant, hardly expressible except through intuition, vague imagery, and a deep sense of compassion and connection. Everything and everyone is a part of everything and everyone else. For a fleeting instant you fall into the vast mirror of the Self, knowing in your bones and nervework its innumerable reflections.

The witness, the observer here, feels rooted in experience yet not fixed and immobile. In fact, this witness senses an actual identification with what is experienced, not only on the surface of things, but somehow also within these things and events.

This "witness," central in yoga, is less harmonious with the models of science. For Bohm there would appear to be some difficulty of extended "awareness" without thought, although thought does phase off into the holoflux and intuition and imagination serve some of this purpose. There is a great unconscious sea of energy, but the "experience" of it is difficult to describe and may be ineffable because the sea is infinite. This sea or field, however, does contain information.

For Pribram, thought and consciousness appear to be a sort of epiphenomenon of the emerging character of the brain. The possibility that the neural network and patterns generate codes that are isomorphic to physical reality, including the implicate order, does not adequately account for the "observer" in this process. We have tried to note that the wave fronts that cross synaptic junctions create stable memory and are themselves subject to observation from another perspective. We are also aware that our ego can be separate from our thoughts. We have indicated that space and time have meaning only in the explicate domain and are collapsed along with our usual sense of distance in the implicate domain. We are led inescapably to "locating" the Self or observer outside of the explicate or space-time domain of which our ego is a part. What happens when the sine wave that generates a wave front is collapsed? It becomes a dimensionless point, outside the extensions of space and time.

We have come to see the Self as beyond the waking ego and yet as its substratum. The ego goes through *modifications*, then disappears during sleep. The Self, however, can be identified fleetingly during introspection while awake and briefly during certain phases of sleep as the "observer" of our sleep. It also appears in states of meditation when pure awareness is experienced. This Self is not part of the wave front of *chitta* or memory, for it observes and utilizes memory. It is not "contained" in space and time for it observes in different space and time sequences. Instead it begins to appear more and more as a dimensionless vibratory event manifesting as pure awareness, which has the characteristics of luminosity, intelligence, and profound peace. It is "located" in the implicate order. Therefore, it is reflected in all other events and it is implicitly aware of all other events in explicate space-time. It is nonlocal in nature.

Accomplished yogis studied while experiencing the Self show greatly slowed pulse rate, no REM, EEG proliferation of theta and delta brainwaves and sometimes high-speed beta waves, and a progressive synchronization of all brainwaves across the whole cortex. One meditator described such a state:

> One remembers having had a body that is located somewhere on the planet, and one used to be able to use one's mind to channel thought, but this seems now like a hoax. Logic seems to be a framework for consciousness trapped in its focus in the *notion* of the self, limiting understanding,

whereas one intuits transcendental logic such as that referred to by Ouspensky in the *New Model of the Universe.*

Others have employed some aspects of this altered state of consciousness for healing. (2)

This experience of the Self, as opposed to the more limited experience of ego, would appear to be capable of separation not only from the five channels of the sensory world but also from the frontal self or personality. This separation is briefly experienced in certain sleep conditions and in *pratayahara.* Because it is an aspect of the human system, the Self is ultimately ahistorical and manifest in all human cultures. It persists through bodily changes but is often hidden behind more transient identities, e.g., race, sex, age, social position, etc.° In truth, it appears, after divorce from these, as the substratum of identity of the human organization that persists through changes in space and time. The personality begins to appear more and more as a series of unfolding potentialities, of particular fleeting permutations of the Self, but not at all exhausting the manifestations of this Self.

This shift in our understanding of personality would seem to imply that personality is a "denser" aspect of the Self. When we focus on the "density" of this energy stratum, we mean it is only one level of energy intensity in a universe replete with many levels of matter-energy manifestation. This denser aspect is involved more completely in the exchange of energy and recurrent transactional patterns between the significant others of the Family Unconscious. The features of the personality, behaviors, attitudes, patterns, habits, dynamisms, etc., whatever you want to call them, are clearly *discrete* in experience. We can often

---

°Depending on what state or even country you're from, you are classified in a certain race e.g. proportion of "ethnic" blood in Antebellum U. S. South and its rabid expression in present-day apartheid South Africa. The DSM III of Psychological disorders has "gender diffusion" as a diagnostic classification; and one can have sex reassignment operations with attendent hormonal treatment.

identify these discrete patterns in ourselves and observe them as they operate and are passed on to others in the family learning context. This does not operate on a conscious level but mostly on an unconscious level.

As the personality emerges in its series of potentialities, the ego is intimately involved. Spontaneous emotions occur as open adaptations to situations and in a sense are a form of direct perception. The ego, however, often then seeks to "own" the experience of the system, therein limiting its range more than necessary. The ego is necessary in the world, as seen in previously outlined reasons. Whether the ego becomes the sole guardian of the personality is another issue.

In healthy adaptation of the personality, there is intimacy and stable permutation of boundaries between persons. The unhealthy boundary situation can be seen in the "borderline" patient's anxious oscillation between emotional isolation and fusion with others. The "borderline" patient poorly manages his *tangible perception* of undivided wholeness. In the extreme situation the clinician can observe the "psychotic insight" of the individual who loses his or her boundaries quickly with an uncanny ability to touch the inner world of others. The great illusion of individuality must not be too quickly annihilated but must be approached carefully, quietly. Needless to say, in successful psychotherapy, both individual and family, this is done as the therapist becomes an aspect of the client's Family Unconscious. Thus again it is extremely helpful for the therapist to use creatively his or her own unconscious and many of its vectors to increase true intimacy and stability.

It is obvious that this Self we are focusing on is not simply the "mental" and egoic aspect of our nature. It would lead us far afield to explore the engagement and gradual disengagement of the Self with its various mental structures, some enduring, some transient, as they unfold through development. An exceptionally lucid description of the Self's involvement with these structures through their developmental stages can be seen in Wilber's perfectly balanced visionary and scientific account. (3)

We mentioned earlier our support for the position that consciousness pervades everything, even the subquantum level. Several other prominent quantum physicists we have not mentioned also see the tangible operation of consciousness on the quantum and subquantum level. (4, 5) In the domain of neurological investigation, Eccles pointed out that the highest reaches of consciousness, termed by him *imagination*, appear to occur when there is a transcendence or emergence out of the wave front flux to a more "resonant-like intensification" of activity in the cortex. Pribram simply refers to some "mechanism as yet unimagined" that would account for the operation and ultimate observation of this flux of wave fronts and holographic processes. Remember that these wave fronts are actually a form of *light* and as such are energy. The Self is an observer of this energy. It is our assertion that this Self is totally outside the domain not only of time and space but also of energy and material manifestation. It is described as the ageless noumenon behind transient phenomena. Energy, ego, and structure undergo constant change; the Self is immanent, changeless, transcendent. This changeless and immanent aspect outside explicate space and time operates on a different logic. As Aurobindo says,

> It is founded on a feeling of all in each and of each in all ... it is an oceanic and ethereal sense in which all particular sense knowledge and sensation is a wave or movement or spray or drop that is yet a concentration of the whole ocean and inseparable from the ocean. (6)

In terms of this observer in the implicate order, it is noted that Pribram asserts that the neuronal systems in the brain reflect the structure of the physical universe. The brain is clearly a material event in space-time and also is a reflection of the organizing principles of our intelligible universe.

While it is possible that the human brain does not reflect
the *only* organizing principles of the universe, it is clear
that it reflects some of these.

As Muktananda points out from his experience:

> Then passing from turiya into sushupti, or deep sleep, he
> takes with him the experience of the turiya state. In deep
> sleep he still sees nothing different from himself. Leaving
> deep sleep and going into the dream state, he becomes his
> own dream world and all the objects of that state—chariots,
> horses, elephants, etc. He discovers that the Witness of the
> deep sleep state is the same as that of dreams. And then,
> passing from the dreaming to the waking state, he realizes
> that the same transcendental Being also underlies that.
> Thus from turiyatita to turiya, turiya to deep sleep, deep
> sleep to dreaming, dreaming to waking, and vice versa,
> only one Witness remains. (7)

This observer is much like the hero in the famous story
of the "Garden of Forking Paths" by Jorge Luis Borges.
Many simultaneous events can be witnessed, all of which
deconstruct our familiar linear time and space sequence.
Similarly, the witness observes the range of his or her own
consciousness, its numerous possibilities and actualizations.
This is no mere play on words with no basis in actuality.
The Schrödinger equation demonstrates the multiple possibilities each millisecond for every particle/wave event
in the explicate order. These possibilities are occurring in
actuality in the implicate order. This is the many-worlds
perspective of quantum physics formulated by Everett and
Wheeler in 1957. (8) They view the universe as continually
splitting, re-emerging, and working through a stupendous
number of possibilities. (The mathematical formulation of
this model is called Hilbert space, an analogue of Euclidean
space, in which a system of orthogonal straight line coordinates is possible. Time is multilayered and crisscrossed.
Consciousness rescues us from the "infinite regress" of
Von Neumann and emerges as the "hidden variable" in
the material world.)

SELF AND PERSONALITY STYLES

It follows from all that we have said that since undivided wholeness and the shared psychological field are basic aspects of both the material/energy world and the mental world, our notions of healthy personality functioning flow from this. The personality's way of handling this unitary process is crucial. As we said earlier, the personality appears more as a series of unfolding potentialities, of fleeting permutations of the Self, but not exhausting its manifestations. The flowering of psychological health is toward integration and an increasing sense of wholeness. Difficulties in this process are seen as blocked attempts in development, as obstructions to transcendence. Various psychological syndromes are seen differently from this perspective.

We have already described the back-and-forth psychological movement of the "borderline" personality in its attempts to integrate powerful patterns around intimacy, fusion, and autonomy in the Family Unconscious. This is a struggle to approach functional wholeness. In the same way the behavior of the "paranoid" individual is an attempt at wholeness and integration.

In many cases of paranoid perception, in order to control anxiety the individual attempts to integrate too many disparate aspects of the world too quickly, and failure ensues. In a life crisis the system is flooded with perceptions it can't smoothly integrate. The paranoid individual may actually sense the real world of multiple interconnections, see and feel many things and events in "reference to himself," but the necessary expansion in personality and ego boundaries is too rapid and he or she falls back to familiar terrain, the ego. The paranoid style is often exquisitely sensitive to family and interpersonal relationships and attends to "data" which is ordinarily "selectively inattended to," including nonverbal and perhaps trans-psychic material. The ego, in defensive style, attempts to "explain" the process but is flooded by fears of dissolution and death, of annihilation of the only stable sense of selfhood it knows, the ego. One can witness the powerful intrusion of destructive fantasy material, perhaps from the root chakra which is focused on concerns with survival. Should the system completely disintegrate, the phenomenon of "psychotic insight" may occur where the system is open and unusually sensitive to other psyches, a situation which occurs often in the psychiatric emergency room, not only in relation to other family members but to the hospital staff.

Thus the paranoid style, failing at wholeness and integration at a higher level, but actually sensing the real undivided wholeness of feeling and psychic influence in the world, falls back into hostile, defensive boundaries, projecting blame and responsibility outward to others. Delusions occur as an attempt to explain the process to the ego. These delusions often contain a grain of truth but are entangled in florid, egocentric symbolism and imagery.

The multiple personality would appear to reflect a different perception and attempt to deal with the fragmentation of undivided wholeness. Research has indicated that the multiple personality has experienced severe trauma in the family constellation. This leads to internal psychological splintering, with the different aspects of the person becoming different "personalities" in an attempt to wall off the pain and cope with the situation. Here we see that more than ego is involved, since many aspects of the personalities that emerge are unconscious and seemingly autonomous. These different personalities also show different EEG patterns, different responses to medication, different electrical skin responses, and even different perceptual styles. (9) Thus, the shattered personality is an indication of a level of multiple processing, potentially within all of us at a very deep level. Some agency, it seems, acts upon the brain and mind to elicit these diverse responses. In its positive expression, this potentiality is a fountainhead of creativity, a pathway of interconnecting worlds and realities.

It appears that this multiple-personality disturbance, this failure to approach undivided wholeness occurs at the causal level of the mind. This level is beyond the unconscious as usually conceived and is indicative of a deeper disorder.

The many-worlds view of quantum mechanics with its Hilbert space of many potential realities is analogous to this process. Here the worlds are continually splitting, etc. The closest most of us come to this world of multiple realities may occur in disturbances of deep dreamless sleep. Here, clinically speaking, slow delta brainwaves predominate and the person upon waking rarely remembers anything except panic, terror, and an other-worldly or "not-me" kind of experience. Hence, these are called "night terrors" to distinguish them from the more common nightmares. At this level, which we hold to be the causal level of the mind, we either integrate in a state of bliss or else experience a terrifying fragmentation and eruption of other worlds into our system.

We will return to this many-worlds concept in the final chapter on the Self. However, from this very brief description we can see how a new conception of psychic energy dynamics and personality styles interlacing the Family Unconscious is implicit in the idea of undivided wholeness and shared affective-ideational fields. A fuller discussion of these three syndromes would take us far afield.

EFFECTS OF DIRECTED CONSCIOUSNESS

Our consciousness can create and manifest certain potentialities by various techniques. The previously mentioned hypnosis and biofeedback techniques can be successful with relatively little practice in a good clinical setting. With prolonged practice over years, however, other areas of the psyche and consciousness come forward. The Self witnesses the play of all of these.

The higher techniques of visualization (*tulpas*) and directed breath control (*pranayama*) lead to an elevation of consciousness difficult to describe. The Self is beyond duality. The wave/particle or wavepacket character of light is taken to be a manifestation of a deeper unity, of which wave and particle are projective aspects. They unfold from that primal sea of light we have discussed. By sustained visualization and concentration, one can effect, over years, a state of consciousness that transcends the play of matter and energy. This state gives one control over the process of perception and all the aspects of the Self that are fused with the "denser" phenomena of matter. (10) Thus, these practices can produce unusual and experimentally measurable physiological changes, such as increasing surface skin temperature at will by 20 degrees (as occurs in the practice of Tum-mo Yoga). (11) Walking on a bed of hot coals without injury, cessation of cardiac functions, significant brainwave alteration, and other demonstrated accomplishments are clearly the more advanced practices. These techniques have been used by peoples all over the earth through various epochs, but have perhaps reached their highest and most systematic expression in some forms of Tantric and Vedantic yoga. Excavations at Harappa and Mohenjodaro in the Indus valley show that these practices were rooted in experimental laboratories that were ancient long before the Aryan invasions of India.

We can observe this vast and intimate process of mind and matter by experiencing the Self. This Self operates through mind, and mind then operates through the body. In other words, we witness the play of the transcendent Self in its operation both with mind and with the four basic interactions or forces of the physical domain presented earlier. We assert that these four interactions can to some extent each be influenced by focused consciousness.

SUMMARY

We have come to see the Self as the substructure of perception in each context of observation. After separation from the different channels of perception, including the intellect and mind, the Self was seen to be the unchanging bedrock that is unmanifest and behind all our actions. It is deeper than our changing social and cultural experiences; indeed it does not appear to undergo modification at all. A different conception of personality functioning and psychic energy dynamics issues from this. Various explorers have described the state to us, and still these "descriptions" fall vastly short of the illimitable experience itself. The experience unifies the experiencer, the process of experience, and object of experience itself. The ego is but a function, in explicate space and time, of this Self that dwells beyond and yet includes it in the implicate order. This implicate order is in touch with all other events in the universe, including all the forces we have spoken of, in addition, naturally, to the Family Unconscious. The Self has come to be seen as a dimensionless vibratory event manifesting as pure awareness and having the characteristics of luminosity, intelligence, and profound peace.

19

Self, Energy, and the Roots
of Transcendence

*One so freed from the bondage of senses transcends all
material relation, and becoming all supreme light, re-
gains his own Self. This indeed is Self. It is beyond
mortality, beyond fear. It is Truth; Truth is only another
name of The Absolute.*

Chandogya Upanishad

Walk into the woods on a bright autumn day. Orange,
brown, and burnished gold leaves repeat everywhere that
nature has moved toward its ritual self-immolation. It occurs
to you as you inhale the cool air that this sea of colors is also
an intimate aspect of your own nature. Yes, we too are
passing away. When does the inanimate oxygen of the air
become that intimate aspect of your consciousness? When
is it no longer a part of your life force? Perhaps everywhere
we are in touch with every force, every affect and event all
the time. Gravity is not limited to the stars and planets but is
felt in our bones and muscles. Electricity animates tele-
communications and huge dynamos and also all of our brain
network. The energies of nature, no matter how subtle or
astronomical, are with us in each breath and permutation
of our lives in some way. Let's look at them closely, one
by one.

The electromagnetic force can be directly influenced by
mind and Self through meditation, hypnosis, and biofeedback procedures. In meditation the conscious progressive

182

synchronization of EEG patterns, which are electromagnetic, leads to increased coherence of wave propagation in the cerebral cortex, and this directly affects the subtle magnetic field associated with all electrical activity. This extends to the activity of the sympathetic and parasympathetic nerve plexuses and chakras. The magnetoencephalogram instrument measures the magnetic field of the cortex and has implications for quantum processes (see Chapter 12).

In psychosomatic syndromes such as chronic muscular pain, tension, and migraine headaches, the organism's reaction to recurrent mental patterns is overt. The mind holds the body's tension in various ways and so can be seen to enfold the body in the process. Such chronic patterns effect nerve conduction, etc., and are therefore partially transmitted by the electromagnetic force. The electromagnetic force appears to be intimately related to the weak interaction or force of the four basic interactions as mentioned earlier. This relationship between the weak interaction and the more familiar electromagnetic force is by way of the gauge symmetry perspective which sees both as really identical processes but mediated by different mass-exchange particles (intermediate vector bosons and photons, respectively. The former is nearly a thousand times smaller than the latter but cannot be dismissed when dealing with such subtle phenomena).

Research in the Soviet Union seems to be much further along in this area. They have apparently mapped many of the ways the electromagntic force interacts with the nervous system, not only of humans but of other life forms on the planet. (1, 2)

The "strong force" appears to be affected in some disturbances of living organisms. (3) Prolonged psychosomatic dysfunctions, e.g., cancer, some stress syndromes and glandular complications, diabetic and biochemical alterations, affect the subtle *molecular processes* of the system and cellular changes occur. While this may be primarily electromagnetic, we note again that in dark-adaptation experiments, which are similar to meditation in that external stimuli are held to a minimum and consciousness is focused, the human retina can consciously perceive a series of two or three photons, which are subatomic particles. A well trained biofeedback subject can selectively activate a single, isolated neuron. The accomplished yogi can create thermal differences in the same hand inches apart by concentration alone. And finally, Patanjali's 40th yoga aphorism states that consciousness reaches from the galaxy to the level of the atom. He made this introspective observation nearly 2500 years ago! Our tools are an extension of our nervous system and at present these highly sensitive and imperfect nervous systems are controlling nuclear reactors all over the planet.

Hasted, an experimental physicist, has measured and replicated the effects of a number of person's concentration on objects in the laboratory. (4) He has uncovered measurable changes in the hardening, softening, and magnetization of metals, thermal alterations in materials, movement of objects from a distance, and numerous other structural changes that involve focused consciousness interacting with different energy fields. He has even reported events that are implicated in trans-spatial and trans-temporal processes. All were seen to be due to the conscious involvement of a gifted subject. These bear witness to the direct effect of consciousness even on the atomic and subatomic level.

The gravitational force of infinite range (because of the exchange of massless particles as in the electromagnetic force) would appear to be intimately related to the bio-gravitational field of Dubrov and others. Examples have already been provided.

It is curious that we often notice the interactions of nature externally before we recognize that these forces are also an intrinsic aspect of our own nature and that we are an integral part of the natural scheme. The simple propagation of electrical force along the nerve axon (by way of the sodium-potassium pump) is one of many examples. It seems that on some level of consciousness we are influenced by and also influence each natural force or interaction of nature. This Self we are examining is involved with all these energies, these shifts and fluctuations in the matrix of reality. Yet it observes these modifications just as it observes the modifications of its own ego. This observer is of the implicate order beyond the projective aspects of particle and wave, matter and force, the channels of space and time. In this implicate order are enfolded all these projective dimensions we utilize to operate in the material world.

We have seen that the human brain has embedded in it many if not all the organizing principles of the material universe and thus reflects the material universe. We suspect that this Self we have been probing reflects the self of *all* self-organizing systems of both the explicit material universe and of the implicate order, including *all* self-organizing systems at each level of operation. The Self in us is also the Self of all else. This is not a reductionist perspective, but rather a true homology. One begins to see the Self in every aspect of material/energy manifestation and beyond.

On the subquantum level we witness principles of self-organization and self-consistency laws, as elucidated by Bohm and Chew in the "new physics." The atomic nucleus has its own system of exchanges, balances, and laws of regulation. The molecular level witnesses cycles of self-organization that lead to perpetuation and *increasing* complexity. The first section of this book mentioned the hypercycles of Eigen and other biochemists looking at the earliest life-like systems on the planet. "Above" these are the organelles, which are self-perpetuating biochemical systems within the cellular structure of all biosystems on earth. The cell itself is a self-regulating, "breathing" system next in this hierarchy. The organ systems reflect self-regulating principles which are a subsystem of the entire body. The ego and personality also form systems, as does the Family Unconscious. Beyond this are our sociobiological and cultural systems, and eventually the ecological and planetary system. The Self participates in and through all these levels of self-organization and yet is not exhausted by them.

We can imagine an explorer like Columbus on the great sea. His sensory experience informs him that space and time are fixed, linear actualities, not curved and variable phenomena. But this Columbus has an intuition, supported by abstract logic and scattered reports of earlier explorers, that suggests to him that indeed the "flat" sea does curve and undergo modifications at the "edges." Slowly this voyager realizes the limits of his vision. We know now how narrow is the frequency band of visible light within the whole electromagnetic spectrum and that below a certain speed of the camera flicker, motion is stilled. Quietly today's observer and voyager realizes the narrow range of the auditory system, how beyond a certain variable pitch nothing is heard. The distilled mind then reads its history and prejudices in the taste sensations it knows, and watches the shadow of this made dim with age. The tactile threshold is slightly different for everyone, and the college student in a psychophysiological class learns how variable and illusory the tactile sense can be. The sense of smell is even more subtle, registering mostly on the primal levels of attraction and repulsion, like and dislike. All this storm, this passing kaleidoscopic impression of the sensory world, is witnessed by our observant modern Columbus. By becoming aware of the limits of his sensory experience, he slowly is able to operate on and transcend these limits. Continual focus on the sea of linear thoughts leads eventually through the vast illusion, so that space and time reveal themselves to be categories of experience, yet not the sole field coordinates of the mind.

Experiments with hypnotic alterations of space and time demonstrate that profound emotional and perceptual changes occur for the individual. When the spatial dimension is increased, often ecstatic feelings are experienced; yet when space or depth is removed, schizophrenic reactions are seen. When time is stopped, a sense of un-reality emerges and spatial distortion occurs. When the time dimension is quickened, a manic feeling pervades. These and other experiences occur when space and time are quickly altered. (5) These changes can be controlled by the process of gradual meditation.

The world-line of the mind in its engagement with denser matter sees these categories of space and time fluctuate, reverse, open and close, and can witness the merging of points that once appeared separated by great distances. This also can be seen in some theorems of the new physics, parapsychological research findings, and our common dreamlife.

At a certain point in our own voyage of discovery duality itself becomes a hindrance. The secret union of all things and events is either suspected or becomes intuitively known. Reason becomes enriched by innumerable inter-connections of logic, imagery, and emergent apprehension. As the voyager's experience dawns into recognizing the Self in all levels and events, duality quietly fades and a profound sense of equanimity emerges.

When we say the Self is not exhausted by the play of matter and energy we are again referring to the implicate order. This implicate order is not a specific "place" in physical reality. In quantum interconnectedness and the process of non-locality of causal events, the integrity of the subsystem, system, and suprasystem is everywhere, as is the Self. As such the Self is inherently non-findable and yet is everywhere manifest. All in each, each in all.

Thus we see that from many sources, some ancient, some modern, the material universe, from the astronomical to the subquantum level, is composed of self-organizing principles and processes that all interpenetrate and partake of the Self.

THE REALMS OF CONSCIOUSNESS

It occurs to us that there is a powerful correspondence between the material and energy universe of quantum-relativistic physics as put forward by Bohm and J. C. Pearce

(6) and the yogic view of matter/energy and the levels of consciousness. We mean here that yogic experience posits four basic states of consciousness. Each state is said to be intimately related to a "body" or sheath of the Self. There is the familiar waking state; the dream state; the state of deep dreamless sleep; and *Turiya* or *Samadhi*. Actually there are subtle levels of *Samadhi*, but verbally differentiating *Turiya* from *Turiyatita* is by definition impossible because both are wordless states of awareness beyond thought.

The waking state corresponds to our physical bodies. The dream state is said to involve the subtle or energy body. Duality still reigns in this state of consciousness. The state of deep sleep without dreaming corresponds to the "causal body," and the state of *Turiya* or *Turiyatita* is involved with the "supracausal body." Each is a state of being, a stabilized vibratory context, expressed through a "body," either physical or existing only at frequency levels. Various techniques of meditation will unfold these enfolded states. Open your eyes and you touch the physical body; lucid dreaming and Yoga Nidra lead to the subtle energy body and beyond. Attempting during meditation to recapture the bliss of deep dreamless sleep will lead to the causal body, while steady meditation and contemplation empty into *Turiya*.

We note that the explicate order is that of observing ego, of the constructive interference patterns of electromagnetic and other energies that manifest as the material world. The implicate order is the energy pattern itself that manifests the explicate order. It bears a certain correspondence to the energy body of dream manifestation. At this level the Self is still identified in the most subtle way with matter and energy. The realm of pure potential energy is the great "quantum sea" of free energy in the universe, the energy represented by every solution of the Schrödinger equation. This energy has enfolded within it consciousness, consciousness associated with a "sheath" or "body" referred to in Yoga as the *causal* body. We have seen that the state of deep, dreamless sleep occasionally has a "witness" which is aware of the many potential states and levels of events. It is aware of the constantly splitting, re-merging, and multilayered universe of space and time. The many-worlds view of quantum mechanics plays here in what can mathematically be termed vectors in Hilbert space. There is no duality here. In the many worlds of Hilbert space the various events of matter and energy do not communicate with each other. Thus our analogy has limits because on the causal level these various worlds are integrated. Here is where the implicate order implies a reality vastly beyond what we call matter. The wave nature of matter, remember, implies an implicate order.

Our notion of space and time has gone through innumerable permutations, leaving any concept of rigid cause-effect behind. Subtle aspects of our nature are dealt with at this level. It was Vivekananda who pointed out that our "fine samskaras are to be conquered by resolving them into their causal state. These samskaras are the subtle impressions which remain even when the mental waves are destroyed by meditation. [The closest most of us come to this level is in the bliss of deep sleep without dreaming.] How can these samskaras be controlled? By *resolving the effect into the cause.* When the *chitta* (memory), which is an effect, is resolved, through *samadhi*, into its cause, *asmita* or 'I-consciousness' [the observer or Self], then only do the five impressions die along with it." (7)

Each level of consciousness with its corresponding "sheath" is a manifestation or projection of a higher order process or suprasystem that incorporates it. Each level has processes unique to it, and these processes manifest laws that, given the nature of gravitational collapse implicit in Relativity theory, may themselves be mutable over duration. (8) The worlds are no longer "in" space and time, but "of" space and time. Anyone gazing at this intricate interplay of energies and laws at different strengths and ranges sees the dance of Shiva in every eye.

Finally the realm above this is that of insight-intelligence, which we might link to the yogic view of pure consciousness, of *Turiya*, of the supracausal body, of the Self. Words cannot quite capture the wordless here and by nature are inaccurate; yet we can say that this is the ground of which material and energy possibility is a subset. That which is experienced as particle or wave, or any energetic and/or mental phenomenon at other levels, is known in its primordial essence to be "That" which exists. It is the primal sea of light energy that is neither particle nor wave and which, while appearing "empty," is so only in the sense of being paradoxically "full" of infinite energy in an organizing intelligent field. In the Eastern view matter and energy phenomena are only two *categories* of what exists, and all that exists is a manifestation of consciousness. Simple inductive reasoning shows that merely because we know matter and energy are both "reality," we are not justified in ruling out all other possible ways for the "reality" to manifest. Another way to express this, albeit still in dualistic terms, is that the "That-ness" is both the material/energy existence *and* its "void" background of an intelligent, organizing field that enfolds all aspects. In other words, "That" comprises both the property of matter/energy in its phenomenal "location" in space and time *and* the "nonlocal" aspect of matter/energy that is everywhere interconnected. Yogis speak of the "pure light" of consciousness experienced between one phenomenon and the next, between one thought and the next.° This state is the realization that since consciousness is everything, it is only veiled by images, senses, and vast, intricate illusions. When the seeker, whether physicist, mystic, or serendipitous

---

°It is interesting to note that there appears to be a relationship between the processes of meditation and death. Slowing down the system so that what is "between" phenomena is revealed and the various techniques of meditation to approach this state have a correspondence with the ultimate disintegration of our material bodies known as "death" and the "clear light of the Dharma-kaya" of the Tibetan yogins (W. Y. Evans-Wentz, *Tibetan Yoga and Secret Doctrines*, London: Oxford University Press, 1958).

poet, "sees" the worlds beyond the senses and the alphabet of waking/dream experience, he or she realizes "I am That."

The Self is rooted here, immanent and all equating. Information transfer at great "distances" directed by the Self becomes malleable. In such a universe events akin to synchronicity and psi are not only explainable, but necessary.

SUMMARY

We began this section with an exploration of the four presently known elementary interactions of the material universe. These interactions involved not only the forces between astronomical occurrences but also between sub-quantum events. From an examination of these interactions we noted the limitations of the present theoretical schemas in organizing the new data presently manifesting through new instruments. Of particular concern were the difficulties encountered in situations of very high energy (greater than 10^9 eV) and small distances (10^{-33} centimeters), and short time durations (10^{-44} seconds). We stressed the particular difficulties with the cognition and experience of light, its measurement, and even the relative structure of matter itself. We saw the endless search for the latest ultimate particle.

This led to a new perspective and re-interpretation of the existing data into a more holonomic paradigm. The holonomic paradigm involved the "undivided wholeness in flowing movement" of the universe and of necessity demanded an exploration of how we are "aware of this undivided wholeness in varying degrees."

We explored the process of the ego and its intimate connection with our process of understanding. Out of this came exploration of the way that data from the internal and external worlds makes itself known to the observer. Certain limitations of the observing ego made it clear that the ego was not the ultimate observer of events in the implicate order and was only partially so in the explicate order.

At this point the nature of light and how it affects our

awareness was explored, not only on a physical level, but also on a neurological level. How the wave fronts are generated by electrical stimulation, vibration, or light, in the body to the neural network and the way that the observer uses the processes of these neural networks were elaborated in some technical detail. Potential ways in which very small degrees of influence by the observer can affect events on a quantum and subquantum level were explored. Eventually it came to be seen that the observer of thought, wave front, and its result or memory, could not be located within space-time, but of necessity had to be located outside space-time in the implicate order.

The implicate and explicate orders were seen to have an uncanny correspondence to yogic models of matter and consciousness. This is an ahistorical perspective since it holds for different peoples and cultures. This led to the realization that the Self is a dimensionless, vibratory event characterized by luminosity, intelligence, and profound peace.

VI

The Common Stream

Some day, after we have mastered the winds, the waves, the tides and gravity, we shall harness for God the energies of love. Then for the second time in the history of the world man will have discovered fire.

Teilhard de Chardin

20

Family Life and Healing

Love is the greatest science we can come to know.
Mother Teresa

Throughout this chronicle of the family and its unconscious loom of thoughts, energies, and affective interconnections, we tried to locate its patterns in the heart of everyday matters. The Thanksgiving dinner, the wedding or funeral of a friend, each such common-place event has the elements that set personal time and meaning in order. Psi is an extraordinary and yet common occurrence in this network.

We have deluged the reader with chapters and references to psi occurrences partly in order to show that this is in line with the new physics and psychology, and yet was intimated thousands of years ago in our ancient poems, texts, and practices. In this final chapter, we want to feel our way back into day-to-day life, even as you, the reader, must do.

That phone call, seemingly out of the blue, from your old classmate just as you looked through and saw him in the yearbook made an impression on you. So did other such accounts of unexpected contacts you've read about like currents that cross and then disperse in some vast sea. However, when your own dream was later described to you in intimate detail by a close friend who recently had gone through the experiences you dreamed about, then you had a strong sense that another communication channel was possible. After hearing about even more such events, you realized something you couldn't explain. Somehow dreams and close emotional ties seem to be a part of a communication process beyond the ordinary.

The Family Unconscious emerged within this study as a field of information and energy that enfolded the lives of any group of people with powerful affective connections, shared history, and recurrent transactions with each other. These people in turn have the unconscious enfolded within themselves. These groups are usually referred to as families. However, this family is really the seed, the primal energy nexus from which almost all other relationships are later derived. Merely saying that each person is an "aspect" of this energy field is not enough. We *experience* this energy field as powerful emotion, imagery, the vortex from which many of our motivations spin out. In the vast majority of cases it is this field of affective-ideational energy of the Family Unconscious that provides a background for psi events to occur.

In its healthy form this field of the Family Unconscious is the taproot of compassion. It is the playground and laboratory of the Self, the place where the innate knowledge that all life is indeed One can be a tangible reality, and we can act and expand accordingly.

The family is where we learn to engage and disengage, where the sense of commitment and integrity spawns. In this context, psi is simply another natural event that testifies to the interconnectedness of all beings and forces of nature.

We spent much time on the implications of non-locality and field interconnectedness, from Einstein to de Broglie, to Bell and Bohm. We reported numerous research findings on psi in the family, in therapy. We amassed much evidence from ancient and modern sources on the vast continuity of the mental and consciousness fields. Some suggestions on their unity were put forward in the last section. Mostly, this field of the Family Unconscious is healthy and strong, and conveys what is positive and necessary in culture. At its high point it prepares the ground for transcendence.

Obviously not all of these Family Unconscious transactions are so healthy. Within reach of all of our lives is a relative or close friend who has been stung by what our society labels mental illness. In the intimate context of family life, the therapist or perceptive family member can observe, and sometimes to their horror, participate in patterns of interaction that lead to mental and emotional impairment. At this point the professional psychotherapist is called. Almost always everyone in the identified patient's system of interaction has some insight into the truth of the matter, yet too often feels helpless to do anything helpful.

In a sense, all guilt is a "negative" reflection of the fact that on the deepest level we *tangibly* realize the undivided wholeness of our lives with significant others; that indeed when we have repeatedly shared intimacy with them, what touches their lives intimately will, in a nonlocal way, influence us. The intense affective-ideational energy we share interconnects us in ways that slip past the guardians of space and time.

ESP in the cradle is as normal and common as the summer grass. When fear and insecurity about psi events enter the family system the ground is set for many kinds of problems. Psi will not occur as commonly as human speech. Nor will one be engulfed simply because a close person occasionally has direct access to his or her mind. All one's privacy and "individuality" will not be lost. These twin fears are at the root of our fear of ESP in ourselves and others. Once such experiences are accepted as easily as any other natural capacity, the collective fear will subside.

Looking at the ways we engage and disengage with each other, at the operation of psi in the Family Unconscious, at our shifting and mutual identities, at the difficulty of measuring where we "end" and another person "begins," at our tangible but subtle connection over vast distances, it is difficult not to see how we are all an intimate aspect of the same field. As the planets are drawn toward each other, as immense stars hold each other on course, as we can feel that same attractive force between and within ourselves and others, it is difficult not to believe on some intuitive level that love is gravity.

CREATIVE USE OF EMOTIONAL ENERGY

The enfolding field of energy and information focused around specific affective themes was developed in the chapter on affective currents and levels of consciousness. We now come to more practical uses of the concept of this field. Kunz and Peper have outlined a number of interactions in such an affective energy field that enhance creativity and decrease negative feelings. (1) The following is an amalgamation of their suggestions and my own.

1. In situations where the field is agitated by anger from someone, instead of quickly returning the anger we can first acknowledge the situation in our own heart and then our reaction to it. Often we can see the ridiculous disproportion between the anger and the precipitating event. A brief moment of reflection is the key here.

2. We can attempt to actually see those aspects of our own personality reflected in the other, especially when we feel angry at him or her. This is not merely fusion with the other person but rather differentiation between our feelings and his or hers and an assessment of our own subtle input into the situation. Who of us has not been angry at someone, only to find upon analysis that what really bothered us in the other person was a habit of thought or behavior we ourselves engage in? In psychotherapy, of course, this is recognized by the therapist to be an instance of counter-transference.

3. This is particularly important in the marital and family constellation. The long-term effects of anxiety and anger on the body are well known. These unhealthy patterns are eventually introjected or taken in by the young family

members and become the basis of their later transactions with the significant others in their lives. These patterns are recurrent and become stabilized over time.

4. Attempting to see ourselves in some degree in each family member will also serve to increase a general context or background of empathy against which themes emerge. Not only is problem solving fostered by this because compromise is much easier, but there is less need for emotional defenses that rigidify the system. The psychic and emotional fields become more permeable. Most families do not need therapy when the family members are able to see themselves in each other. They relate with humor and compassion despite the usual problems.

5. These simple approaches can be made by each of us while we operate on various levels of experience in the family. Remember that we are made up of fields of affective-ideational energy: the emotional level that operates primarily at the first, second, and third plexus levels; the fourth level of compassion and empathy; the fifth level of creativity; the sixth level of intuitive understanding. (See Chapter 12.) Each level can be brought to a higher state of sensitivity if we look at its characteristics. Kunz and Peper elaborate other ways of increasing the healing process at these levels. Anger radiates, as does love. Both are powers that deeply and intimately affect the body on all levels. We can learn to use love consciously for healing. The perspective is one in which we radiate out and through our field to other fields. The interface between fields of different individuals is our common life. Remember, more often in psychological disturbances it is *who* is the matter with us rather than *what* is the matter with us.

6. It is possible to establish a climate at home in which it is natural to talk with each other about dreams. This will deepen intimacy. It will increase harmony and differentiation at the same time, for all the reasons cited above. A certain shared culture and mythology will arise.

7. Finally, it is extremely helpful to recognize that all is in all. This means that each thought or energy and its opposite

are both embedded in the same root. We have seen that
emptiness and infinite energy are nonlocated in the same
place. In dreams and in some old words of many languages,
things can be transformed to mean their opposite. Love and
hate are obviously close. It is extremely helpful to attempt
to see the "opposite" in an emotional situation. For example,
guilt has embedded in it the sense of deep relatedness to
others, and its resolution leads toward self-forgiveness and
self-acceptance. In anger is rooted the sense of conviction.
Embedded in loss, sorrow, and grief are gratitude and the
recognition of the inescapability of change in the phenomenal world. This leads to seeing the unchangeable Self
behind the changing world of emotional pain, insecurity,
and transience. Paradoxically, in transience is rooted
transcendence.

It is easy to see how the "opposite" emotion or thought
can be recognized and potentially integrated into the nexus
of the family situation. In working with family dynamics it
is much easier to create or amplify an emotion than to
deny it. Eventually a "positive" emotion will replace or
dominate another. This approach is based, not on cold
analytical detachment, but on compassionate transcendence. When we come to see each aspect of the
dynamic as a mirror of ourselves, we come to operate
upon it much better, just as a child must first identify
with his or her hand before detaching from it in order to
use it as an instrument.

THE FAMILY AND THE UNFOLDING SELF

By now it is clear that this perspective contains different
assumptions about the Self. Beyond the various methods of
evolving this Self is the idea that each person in the family
situation is already "perfect" in his or her implicate nature
and that the family's principle goal is to help "remove"
the obstacles to its unfolding. Each member's function is to
help cultivate emotions and insight as a way of life. Each
member is also unfolding and acting out his or her own
particularization of the greater Family Unconscious field.

The paradox is that as each strives to do this, more individuality and differentiation is fostered, even as the family collectively looks toward their shared identity. Unity in diversity, diversity while seeking unity.

In this context psi emerges as simply one more way of experiencing the transcendent unity in the emerging diversity. An increase in psi appears to be occurring in humanity in general, and some nations at present appear to be actively supporting its development. (2) This is a world-wide phenomenon. However, the cultivation of such capacities depends intimately on the family attitude and the attitude of the culture toward such phenomena. In *all* these countries researchers are deeply concerned about the possible military perversion of these abilities.

Increasing recognition and acceptance of psi in family and other contexts is only additional testament to this immense change occurring in our species, whether we like it or not. (3) When the family system begins to cultivate this unfolding, the radical shift we presently witness our species undergoing will quicken. Our species may require it for survival. Given our present technological state with weapons of mass destruction less than ten minutes away and our increasing and innumerable interconnections in the "global village," we find our evolutionary crisis demands that either we love each other or die. Thus we must personally and collectively respond to the crisis. This includes the family. As the bedrock of unity in all aspects and levels becomes inculcated, as compassion is recognized to be the taproot of all feeling and power, the ground is prepared for a naturally meditative state to develop. The unfolding Self through all its personality motivations, within all its cognitive structures and shifting frames, in all its daily activities, will come to seek and experience unity and, paradoxically, emptiness.

It will be natural, upon reflection at each level, to actually know emptiness and at the same time to be in intimate touch with the source of infinite energy and light. The material world is everywhere interconnected, infinite, and empty. Reflection on the sensory world, on transient feelings of all kinds, reveals a euphoric emptiness. Quieting the mental waves exposes peace and equanimity everywhere and in everything. Putting to rest fine discrimination and subtle judgment leads to unspeakable bliss. The focus on pure consciousness reveals emptiness, infinite energy, intelligence, and light. The four basic forces or interactions presently known will some day appear feeble in comparison to the energies of nature of which we have yet to become conscious and master.

The ego develops here as a keen tool only, a translucent container that quietly dissolves over time as one opens to all else. The ego need not shut out our intimations of the Self, of the One, but can serve as a focus for the limitless sea of light in the everyday world of space and time. Eventually everything is recognized as a luminous modification of the Self. This can occur not only in a protected, secluded state away from all others, cloistered in monasteries, murmuring in an ancient tongue, but while eating ice cream with your child or friend, watching the Staten Island ferry go west.

Epilogue

What does not begin cannot end. There is only pulsation, manifestation, interpenetrating awareness and force. We have come full cycle and now can plunge more deeply into the source. The crucible of our individual psyche is inexorably implicated with each other psyche. Those we "know" and resonate with more intensely by intimate and family association spread a matrix that exists within and between us, interlacing us all in an enfolding field, in a Family Unconscious. This in turn interweaves with a vaster unconscious that collects in a vortex of meanings and events. In our more sublime and creative moments we pass from this field and arch briefly into that more resonant intensity of the superconscious. Yet this need not be a transient occurrence, a trailing light we know only through the dream. It can be cultivated by logic and the discipline of a science such as yoga or other meditation, or even using the new physics, *sustained intuition* and a methodology for incorporating this into the body. Above all, with a belief in the limitlessness of our own consciousness, we can move from these cycles of matter, mentation, and energy to the greater ranges of pure consciousness.

As it dawns on the observer, the experiencing principle, that the material/phenomenal "things" we see are a functional construction of the sensory channels and thought structures, that in reality these "things" are a succession of events in space-time, we begin to experience our primordial identity outside the categories of space and time. Just as the Self begins to dis-identify with the succession of thoughts and mental structures and dwells increasingly more fully in the realm of all-embracing and interpenetrating consciousness, we begin to be embraced by all else, and profound waves of compassion sweep through the Self. This is not regression to earlier modes of consciousness, but rather the flowering of development to more inclusive and expansive realms.

Mechanism and atomism lead inescapably to a sense of isolation in a dead universe, to an "epistemological loneliness" that is not cancelled by passion or reason. This is an illusion. There is nothing ultimately separate from us in this world or any other. We are not some stray particle lost within the vast chamber of an ancient heart, but each a rare jewel cast into the light and design of an illimitable art.

Psi episodes, fields of the Family Unconscious, and the innumerable network connecting all from millisecond to millisecond are not mere abstractions, but part of the very stuff of existence. An overarching field enfolds each of us directly and intimately. Space and time become our tools again, releasing us from the tomb of matter. This realization is the Copernican revolution of our era. It will lead inevitably to a re-evaluation, not only of the limits and boundaries of the life-force, but also of the meaning of death. Matter on more and more subtle levels emerges as a form of gravitationally enfolded light. As we still and distill our vital system we become aware of "the Sun dwelling in darkness" (Rig Veda, III, 39.5). The gradual awakening, not by fantasy, but by a timeless science and intuition leads us inescapably to the witness that we are luminous beings. From dust to dust, but also from air to air and light to light do we go. $E = MC^2$ is not the exclusive domain of the bomb and nuclear reactor, but dwells within us as part of our nature and an inevitable stationway in the evolution of consciousness. The universe exists about us and within us. If we look deeply we shall claim our inheritance.

APPENDIX A
The Biological Aspects of Psi Plasma

The physiological changes induced by the administration of carbon dioxide have been ably analyzed by Ernst Gellhorn, and the following sections are quoted from his book, *Physiological Foundations of Neurology and Psychiatry*, (Minneapolis: University of Minnesota Press, 1953), Chap. 19, p. 450 ff.

The action of carbon dioxide on the cortex of the brain has been studied in man through the use of sensory tests. Thus it was found that visual functions decline reversibly in hypercapnea. This is indicated by the increase in the threshold for the discrimination of brightness and by the lengthening of the latent period of the negative afterimages. The effect occurs a few minutes after the inhalation of carbon dioxide in concentrations of 5-7%. Similarly the threshold for hearing rises under these conditions.

It is well known that carbon dioxide increases the frequency and decreases the amplitude of cortical potentials as noted in the human EEG and direct recordings from the cortex of animals. This phenomenon is similar to the changes in the EEG seen during mental activity or sensory stimulation and appears to be primarily due to an excitation which results in a *decreased synchrony* of cortical potentials.

Cortical excitability depends on at least two systems, the long efferent tracts, which send impulses to the specific projection areas, and the hypothalamus, which through its 'upward discharge' influences the cerebral cortex as a whole. The experiments already discussed, and the following observations show that these two systems are influenced by carbon dioxide in opposite ways . . . .

1. The increase in frequency of cortical strychnine spikes occurring during the inhalation of 10% carbon dioxide is due to sub-cortical discharges.

2. If sub-cortical discharges are eliminated, the effect of carbon dioxide on the cortex results solely in a decrease in excitability.

3. Sub-cortical discharges account for the increased responsiveness in hypercapnea of the cerebral mantle to nociceptive and proprioceptive excitation.

The sub-cortical discharge responsible for these phenomena originate in the posterior hypothalamus, since lesions in this area abolish increased spike frequency to carbon dioxide and reduce or eliminate the generalized excitation of the cortex following nociceptive stimulation.

Two facts stand out from these investigations. First carbon dioxide has at least two points of attack in its action on the brain; it diminishes (in concentrations of 10-15%) cortical excitability, as indicated by the reduced responsiveness of sensory projection areas to specific afferent impulses and of the motor cortex to electrical stimulation, and it increases the discharges and reactivity of the hypothalamic-cortical system. This differential action of carbon dioxide is retained in anesthetic concentrations, which eliminate spontaneous hypothalamic and cortical potentials, whereas the responsiveness of specific projection areas persist in a somewhat reduced degree.

Second, this work confirms, on the basis of different experimental procedures, the conclusions arrived at earlier: 1) That awareness is abolished when the hypothalamic-cortical system is anatomically or functionally eliminated. 2) That perception, which is absent in high carbon-dioxide as well as in barbiturate anesthesia, is only possible if afferent discharges to the cortex persist from peripheral receptors and from the hypothalamus.

In Gellhorn's book *Physiological Foundation* Meduna describes the effect of CO_2 on a single nerve:

1. Raises threshold of stimulation (5% CO_2) and increases membrane potential (inc. membrane potential 5.3-6.6MV)

2. Decreases speed of condition of impulses
3. Increases height and duration of action potential
4. Increases resistance to fatigue—CO_2 increases ability to perform work.

APPENDIX B
Four Types of Interaction

Four types of interaction or Force are believed to account for all physical phenomena. "Range" is the distance beyond which the interaction effectively ceases to operate. In two cases this range is infinite and also subject to direct human experience, i.e., gravity and the electromagnetic force. "Strength" is a dimensionless number that characterizes the strength of the force under current conditions of observation. If we make the strong force equal to one, all the others are in reference to it. The gravitational force is then 39 orders of magnitude weaker than the strong force.

FORCE	RANGE	STRENGTH	PARTICLES EXCHANGED	PHYSICAL REACTIONS
Gravity	Infinite	5.9×10^{-39}	Gravitons	Acts on everything in the universe: Astronomical to sub-quantum.
Electro-Magnetic	Infinite	10^{-2}	Photons	Chemical Systems
Strong	10^{-13}-10^{-14} cm	$\cong 1.0$	Gluons	Nuclear Reactions
Weak	« 10^{-14} cm	1.02×10^{-5}	Intermediate Vector Bosons (w^+, w^-, z)	Radioactivity

Notes

CHAPTER 1

1. S. Freud, *The Interpretation of Dreams*, (New York: Avon Books, [1900] 1965), p. 78.

2. B. B. Wolman, *The Unconscious Mind: The Meaning of Freudian Psychology*, (Englewood Cliffs, NJ: Prentice-Hall, Inc., 1968).

3. C. G. Jung, "The Concept of the Collective Unconscious," from *Archetypes and the Collective Unconscious, Collected Works*, R. F. C. Hull, trans., Bollingen Series XX, (Princeton, NJ: Princeton University Press, 1928), vol. 9, pp. 87-110.

4. _____. "The Personal and Collective Unconscious," *Collected Works* (1935), vol. 7, pp. 202-95.

5. M. B. Smith, "Perspectives on selfhood," *American Psychologist*, 33:12, 1978.

6. J. Piaget, *The Origins of Intelligence in Children*, (New York: W. W. Norton and Co., [1952] 1963).

7. _____. *Play, Dreams and Imitation in Childhood*, (New York: W. W. Norton and Co., [1951] 1962).

8. H. S. Sullivan, *The Interpersonal Theory of Psychiatry*, (New York: W. W. Norton and Co., 1953).

9. J. L. Framo, "Symptoms from a family transactional viewpoint," in N. W. Ackerman, J. Dieb, and J. K. Pearce, eds., *Family Therapy in Transition*, (Boston: Little, Brown & Co., 1970).

10. M. Bowen, "A family concept of schizophrenia," in D. D. Jackson, ed., *Etiology of Schizophrenia*, (New York: Basic Books, 1960).

11. F. J. Dyson, "Field Theory," in *Particles and Fields: Readings from Scientific American*, (San Francisco: W. H. Freeman & Co., [1953] 1980), p. 18.

12. J. C. Sonne, "Entropy and family therapy," paper delivered at Sixth International Congress of Psychotherapy, London, August 4, 1964.

13. M. H. Erickson, In J. Haley, *Uncommon Therapy*, (New

York: Ballantine Books, 1973), p. 24-25.

14. R. D. Hess and G. Handel, "The family as a psychosexual organization," *Family Worlds*, (Chicago: University of Chicago Press, 1959).

15. N. W. Ackerman, *The Psychodynamics of Family Life*, (New York: Basic Books, 1957).

16. A. Haley, *Roots: Saga of an American Family*, (New York: Doubleday, Inc., 1977).

CHAPTER 2

1. S. Farber, *Identical Twins Reared Apart: A Re-Analysis*, (New York: Basic Books, 1980).

2. _____. "Telltale behavior of twins," *Psychology Today*, January, 15:1, 1981, 58-80.

3. C. Holden, "Identical twins raised apart," *Science*, 207, 1980, 1323-1328.

4. G. Claridge, S. Canter, and W. Hume, *Personality Differences and Biological Variations: A Study of Twins*, (Elmsford, NY, Pergamon Press, 1973).

5. M. K. McClintock, "Menstrual synchrony and suppression," *Nature*, vol. 229, January, 1971.

6. R. Moody, *Life After Life*, (New York: Bantam Books, 1976).

7. S. M. Sabom, *Recollections of Death: A Medical Investigation*, (New York: Harper and Row, 1982).

8. S. Aurobindo, *The Life Divine*, (Pondicherry, India: All India Press, 1973).

9. A. I. Oparin, *The Origin of Life*, (New York: Macmillan Publishing Co., Inc., 1953).

10. M. Eigen and P. Schuster, *The Hypercycle*, (Heidelberg and New York: Springer-Verlag, 1979).

11. R. Sheldrake, *A New Science of Life: The Hypothesis of Formative Causation*, (Los Angeles: J. P. Tarcher, Inc., 1982).

12. W. McDougall, "Fourth report on a Larmarckian experiment," *British Journal of Psychology*, 28, 1938, 321-345.

13. F. A. Crew, "A repetition of McDougall's Larmarckian experiment," *Journal of Genetics*, 33, 1936, 61-101.

14. W. E. Agar, F. H. Drummond, O. W. Tiegs, and M. M. Gunson, "Fourth report on a test of McDougall's Larmarckian experiment on his training of rats," *Journal of Experimental Biology*, 31, 1954, 307-321.

15. A. Holden and P. Singer, *Crystals and Crystal Growing*, (London: Heinemann, 1961).

16. L. Watson, *Lifetide: The Biology of Consciousness*, (New York: Simon and Schuster, 1980).

17. J. Hasted, *The Metal-Benders*, (London: Routledge and Kegan Paul, 1981).

18. A. R. Coulton, *Kundalini West*, (Glendale, CA: ARC Publishing Co., 1978).

19. Y. Ramacharaka, *Fourteen Lessons in Yoga Philosophy*, (Chicago: Yogi Publication Society, 1903).

20. D. T. Suzuki, *Outlines of Mahayana Buddhism*, (New York: Schocken Books, 1963).

CHAPTER 3

1. N. W. Ackerman, *The Psychodynamics of Family Life*.

2. E. Erickson, *Childhood and Society*, (New York: W. W. Norton, 1950).

3. H. S. Sullivan, *The Interpersonal Theory of Psychiatry*.

4. J. Piaget, *Plays, Dreams and Imitations in Childhood*, (New York: W. W. Norton, 1962).

5. S. Freud, *The Interpretation of Dreams*.

6. I. Markowitz, G. Taylor, and E. Bokert, "Dream Discussion as a means of reopening blocked familial communication," *Psychotherapy and Psychosomatics*, 16:6, 1968, 348-365.

7. N. W. Ackerman, *Psychodynamics of Family Life*.

8. J. L. Framo, "Symptoms from a family transactional viewpoint," in C. Sager and H. S. Kaplan, eds., *Progress in Group and Family Therapy*, (New York: Brunner/Mazel, 1972).

9. E. S. Heath and H. A. Bascal, "A Method of group psychotherapy at the Tavestock Clinic," *International Journal of Group Psychotherapy*, 1968, 18.

10. M. H. Erickson, in J. Haley, *Uncommon Therapy*, (New York: Ballantine Books, 1973), p. 24-25.

CHAPTER 4

1. P. I. Garfield, "Keeping a longitudinal dream record," *Psychotherapy: Theory, Research and Practice*, 10:3, 1973.

2. J. Klugman, "Enmeshment and fusion," *Family Process*, 15:3, September, 1976.

3. L. B. Fierman, *Effective Psychotherapy: The Contribution of Hellmuth Kaiser*, (London: Collier Macmillan Publishers, 1965).

4. E. Greenleaf, "Senoi dream groups," *Psychotherapy: Theory, Research and Practice*, 10:3, 1973.

CHAPTER 5

1. D. Shapiro, A. B. Crider, and B. Tursky, "Differentiation of an autonomic response through operant reinforcement," *Psychosomatic Science*, I, 1964, 147-148.

2. J. Kamiya, "Conscious control of brainwaves," *Psychology Today*, I, April 1968, 55-60.

3. B. T. Engel, "Clinical applications of operant conditioning techniques in the control of the cardiac arrhymthias," *Seminar in Psychiatry*, 5, 1973, 433-438.

4. E. G. Blanchard, L. D. Young, M. R. Haynes and M. D. Kallman, "A simple feedback system for the self-control of bloodpressure," *Perceptual Motor Skills*, 39, 1974, 891-898.

5. J. V. Basmajian, "Control and training of individual motor units," *Mind/Body Integration: Essential Readings in Biofeedback*, (New York and London: Plenum Press, 1979).

6. E. E. Fetz and D. V. Finocchio, "Operant conditioning of specific patterns of neural and muscular activity," *Science*, 174, 1971, 431-435.

7. V. F. Harrison and O. A. Mortenson, "Identification and voluntary control of single motor unit activity in the tibialis anterior muscle," *Anatomical Records*, 144, 1962, 109-116.

8. S. Krippner, *Human Possibilities*, (Garden City, NY: Anchor Press, Doubleday, 1980), pp. 250-51.

9. V. U. Hunt, "A study of structural integration from neuromuscular energy field and emotional approaches," publication of Rolf Institute, Boulder, CO, 1977.

10. H. S. Burr, *The Fields of Life*, (New York: Ballantine, 1973).

11. I. Veith, *The Yellow Emperor's Classic of Internal Medicine*, (Berkeley, CA: University of California Press, [1949] 1972).

12. J. White and S. Krippner, eds., *Future Science: Life Energies and the Physics of the Paranormal*, (Garden City, NY: Anchor Books, 1977), pp. 550-555.

13. U. M. Inyushin, "Bioplasma: A Fifth State of Matter?" in *Future Science*.

14. Ibid.

15. A. P. Dubrov, "Biogravitation and Psychotronics," *Impact of Science on Society*, vol. 24, 1974, 4.

16. K. Trincher and A. Dudoladov, "Spin-lattice interaction of water and protein membranes in cell metabolism," *Journal of Theoretical Biology*, 34, 1972, 557.

17. U. M. Inyushin, "Bioplasma: A Fifth State of Matter?"

CHAPTER 6

1. A. Lowen, *Language of the Body*, (New York: Macmillan, 1971).

2. W. Reich, *Character Analysis*, (New York: Farrar, Straus and Giroux, [1949] 1971).

3. S. Rama, R. Ballentine, A. Hymes, *Science of Breath*, (Honesdale, PA: Himalayan International Institute, 1979).

4. Klein and Armitage, "Nostril cycle and possible relationship to nasal cycle," *Science*, vol. 204, June 22, 1979.

5. E.Funk, "Biorhythms and the breath," *Research Bulletin of the Himalayan Institute*, Winter 1980, 5-8.

6. E. Green and A. Green, "The Ins and Outs of Mind-Body Energy," *World Book Science Annual*, (Chicago: Field Enterprises Educational Corp., 1973).

7. J. Funderbunk, *Science Studies Yoga: A Review of Physiological Data*, (Honesdale, PA: Himalayan International Institute, 1977).

CHAPTER 7

1. L. E. Rhine, *ESP in Life and Lab*, (New York: Collier Books, Macmillan, 1967) p. 204.

2. *Ibid*, p. 144.

3. J. B. Rhine, *Extrasensory Perception*, (Boston: Society for Psychic Research, 1934) (Republished by Branden Press, 1964).

4. _____. *New World of the Mind*, (New York: William Morrow and Co., 1953).

5. L. E. Rhine, *ESP in Life and Lab*.

6. C. Evans, "Parapsychology - What the questionnaire revealed," *New Scientist*, January 25, 1973.

7. S. Schacter and J. E.Singer, *Psychological Review*, 69, 1962, 379.

8. G. R. Schmeidler and R. A. McConnell, *ESP and Personality Patterns*, (Westport, CT: Greenwood Press, [1958] 1973).

9. J. Palmer, "Scoring in ESP tests as a function of belief in ESP, Part I. The Sheep-goat effect," *Journal of the American Society for Psychic Research*, 65, 1971, 373-408.

10. W. Nielsen, "Relationships between precognition scoring level and mood," *Journal of Parapsychology*, 34, 1970, 93-116.

11. J. C. Carpenter, "Intrasubject and subject-agent effects in ESP experiments," in B. Wolman, ed., *Handbook of Parapsychology*, (New York: Van Nostrand Reinhold, 1977).

12. J. M. Bevan, "The relation of attitude to success of ESP

scoring," *Journal of Parapsychology,* 11, 1947, 296-309.

13. J. Palmer "Attitudes and personality traits in experimental ESP research," in *Handbook of Parapsychology.*

14. R. E.White, "The influence of the experimenter, motivation, attitudes and methods of handling subjects in psi test results," in *Handbook of Parapsychology.*

15. E. D. Dean, "The Plethysmograph as an indicator of ESP," *Journal of the American Society for Psychical Research,* 41, 1962, 351-353.

16. C. Tart, "Possible physiological correlates of psi cognition," *International Journal of Parapsychology,* 5, 1963, 375-386.

17. W. Stekel in B. E. Schwarz, *Psychic-Nexus,* (New York: Van Nostrand Reinhold Co., 1980).

18. D. T. Burlingham, "Child analysis and the mother," *Psychoanalytic Quarterly,* 5, 1935, 69-92.

19. J. Ehrenwald, "Mother-child symbiosis: cradle of ESP," *Psychoanalytic Review,* 58, 1971, 455-466.

20. R. G. Standford and B. Mayer, "Relaxation as a psi-conducive state: a replication and exploration of parameters," *American Society for Psychical Research,* 68, 1974, 182-191.

21. A. Puharich, *Beyond Telepathy,* (Garden City, NY: Anchor Books, 1973).

22. S. Krippner, "Experimentally-induced telepathic effects in hypnosis and non-hypnosis groups," *Journal of the American Society for Psychical Research,* 62, 1968, 387-398.

23. T. Moss, M. Paulson, A. Chang, and M. Levitt, "Hypnosis and ESP: A controlled experiment," *American Journal of Clinical Hypnosis,* 13, 1970, 45-56.

24. K. Keeling, "Telepathic transmission in hypnotic dreams," *Journal of Parapsychology,* 35, 1971, 330-331.

25. L. W. Brand and W. G. Brand, "Further studies of relaxation as a psi-conducive state," *Journal of the American Society for Psychical Research,* 68, 1974, 229-245.

26. J. Eisenbud, *Psi and Psychoanalysis,* (New York: Grune and Stratton, 1970).

27. G. Devereux, *Psychoanalysis and the Occult,* (New York: International Universities Press, 1953).

28. F. Capra, *The Tao of Physics,* (Boulder, CO: Shambhala Publications, 1975).

29. J. H. M. Whiteman, "Parapsychology and physics," in *Handbook of Parapsychology.*

CHAPTER 8

1. L. E. Rhine, "Research method with spontaneous cases," in *Handbook of Parapsychology.*

2. G. Murphy, *Challenge of Psychical Research,* (New York: Harper-Colophan Books, 1961).

3. N. W. Ackerman, *The Psychodynamics of Family Life.*

4. R. D. Hess and G. Handel, "The family as a psychosocial organization," *Family Worlds,* (Chicago: University of Chicago Press, 1959).

5. D. Jackson, "The study of the family," *Family Process,* 4, 1965, 1-20.

6. S. Fleck, "An approach to family pathology," in *Manual of Child Psychopathology,* B. Wolman, ed., (New York: McGraw-Hill, 1972).

7. C. A. Whitaker, "The symptomatic adolescent—an AWOL family member," in *The Adolescent in Group and Family Therapy,* M. Sugar, ed., (New York: Brunner/Mazel Publishers, 1975), pp. 202-215.

8. T. Lidz, "The intrafamilial environment of the schizophrenic patient: VI The transmission of irrationality," AMA Archives of *Neurological Psychiatry,* 79, 1958, 305-316.

9. L. Wynne, "Pseudomutality in the family relations of schizophrenics," *Psychiatry,* 21, 1958, 205-220.

10. L. Wikler, "Folie a family: A family therapist's perspective," *Family Process,* 9:3, 1980, 257-268.

11. I. Boszormenyi-Nagy, "A theory of relationships: experience and transaction," in I. Boszormenyi-Nagy and J. Framo, eds., *Intensive Family Therapy: Theoretical and Practical Aspects,* (New York: Harper and Row Publishers, 1965), pp. 33-86.

12. M. H. Erickson in J. Haley, *Uncommon Therapy.*

13. J. Ehrenwald, "Parapsychology and the seven dragons: a neuropsychiatric model of psi phenomena," in G. R. Schmeidler, ed., *Parapsychology,* (American Society for Psychical Research, 1976).

14. M. Ullman, S. Krippner, and A. Vaughan, *Dream Telepathy,* (New York: Macmillan Publishing Co., 1973).

15. _____. "Psi communication through dream sharing." Proceedings of the Parapsychology Foundation, Vancouver Meeting, 1979.

16. J. Eisenbud, *Psi and Psychoanalysis,* (New York: Grune and Stratton, 1970).

17. J. Ehrenwald, *New Dimensions of Deep Analysis*, (New York: Grune and Stratton, 1955).

18. G. Pederson-Krag, "Telepathy and repression," *Psychoanalytic Quarterly*, 16, 1947, 61-68.

19. S. Freud, "Dreams and the Occult," *New Introductory Lectures on Psychoanalysis* (New York: Norton, 1933), Chapter 2.

20. A. Puharich, *Beyond Telepathy*, (Garden City, Anchor Books, 1973), p. 15-16.

21. L. E. Rhine, *ESP in Life and Lab*, p. 13.

22. Ibid, p. 146.

23. K. Osis and E. Bokert, "ESP and changed states of consciousness induced by meditation," *Journal of the American Society for Psychical Research*, 65, 1971, 17-65.

24. H. Durkham and K. R. Rao, "Meditation and ESP scoring," in W. G. Roll, ed., *Research in Parapsychology*, (Metuchen, NJ: Scarecrow Press, 1973).

25. S. Vivekananda, *Raja Yoga*, (New York: Ramakrishna-Vivekananda Center, 1955).

26. L. E. Rhine, *ESP in Life and Lab*, p. 189-90.

27. Ibid, p. 3.

28. B. E. Schwarz, *Psychic-Nexus*, (New York: Van Nostrand Reinhold Co., 1980).

CHAPTER 9

1. R. M. Jones, *The New Psychology of Dreaming*, (New York: Viking Press, 1970).

2. W. Dement and N. Kleitman, "Cyclic variations in EEG during sleep and their relation to eye movement, body motility and dreaming," *Electroencephalography and Clinical Neurophysiology*, 9, 1957, 673-690.

3. A. Rechtschaffen, P. Verdone, and J. Wheaton, "Reports of mental activity during sleep," *Canadian Psychiatric Association Journal*, 8, 1963, 409-414(a).

4. R. T. Pivak, "Mental activity and phasic events during sleep," (Doctoral Dissertation, Stanford University), Ann Arbor, Michigan: University Microfilms, 1971), no. 71-19746.

5. D. Foulkes and G. Vogel, "Mental activity at sleep onset," *Journal of Abnormal Psychology*, 70, 1965, 231-243.

6. E. Green, A. Green, and D. Walter, "Voluntary control of internal states: Psychological and physiological," *Journal of Transpersonal Psychology*, II:2, 1970.

7. G. W. Vogel, B. Barrowclough, and D. Giesler, "Limited discriminability of REM and sleep onset reports and its psychiatric implications," *Archives of General Psychiatry*, 26, 1972, 449-456.

8. S. Rama, R. Ballentine, and S. Ajaya, *Yoga and Psychotherapy: The Evolution of Consciousness*, (Honesdale, PA: Himalayan Institute Press, 1976).

9. M. Ullman, S. Krippner, and A. Vaughan, *Dream Telepathy*, (New York: Macmillan Publishing Co., 1973).

10. J. Ehrenwald, "Parapsychology and the seven dragons: a neuropsychiatric model of psi phenomena," in G. R. Schmeidler, ed., *Parapsychology*, (American Society for Psychical Research, Inc., 1976).

11. Patanjali, quoted in R. Mishra, *The Textbook of Yoga Psychology*, (New York: Julian Press, 1967).

12. S. Vivekananda, *Raja Yoga*, (New York: Ramakrishna-Vivekananda Center, 1955), pp. 181-82.

13. G. Krishna, *Kundalini: The Evolutionary Energy in Man*, (Boulder, CO: Shambhala Press, 1967).

14. B. Bagchi and M. Wenger, "Electrophysiological correlates of some yoga exercises," *Electroencephalography and Clinical Neurophysiology*, supp. 7, 1957, 132-149.

15. J. P. Banquet, "Spectral analysis of EEG in meditation," *Electroencephalography and Clinical Neurophysiology*, 35, 1973, 143-151.

16. E. Peper and S.Ancoli, "The two endpoints of an EEG continuum of meditation," in E. Peper, S. Ancoli, and M. Quinn, eds., *Mind/Body Integration*, (New York: Plenum Press, 1979).

17. M. Reite and J. Zimmerman, "Magnetic phenomena of the central nervous system" *Annual Review of Biophysical Bioengineering*, vol. 7, 1978, 167-168.

18. L. Kaufman and S. Williamson, "The evoked magnetic field of the human brain," *Annals of the New York Academy of Sciences*, vol. 340, May 1980, 45-65.

19. S. Rama, *Enlightenment Without God*, (Honesdale, PA: Himalayan International Institute Press, 1982).

20. K. Pribram, "The neurophysiology of remembering," *Scientific American*, 1969, 73-86.

21. D. Bohm, "The enfolding-unfolding universe," *Re-Vision: A Journal of Knowledge and Consciousness*, Summer/Fall, 1978, 25-51.

22. M. Ullman, "Psi communication through dream sharing," *Proceedings of the Parapsychology Foundation, Vancouver Meeting*, 1979, p. 202.

CHAPTER 10

1. J. S. Bolen, *The Tao of Psychology: Synchronicity and the Self*, (New York: Harper and Row, 1979).

2. C. G. Jung, "Synchronicity: An acausal connecting principle," *Collected Works*, vol. 8, 1973.

3. J. Piaget, *Play, Dreams and Imitation in Childhood*, (New York: W. W. Norton & Co., 1962).

4. _____. *The Origins of Intelligence in Children*, (New York: W. W. Norton & Co., 1963).

5. E. D. Dean, "The plethysmograph as an indicator of ESP," *Journal of the American Society for Psychical Research*, 41, 1962, 351-353.

6. E. D. Dean and C. B. Nash, "Coincident plethysmograph results under controlled conditions," *Journal of the American Society for Psychical Research*, 44, 1967, 1-13.

7. H. Motoyama, "An electrophysiological study of Prana (Ki)," *Journal for Research for Religion and Parapsychology*, 4:1, November 1978.

8. S. Aurobindo, *The Life Divine*, (Pondicherry, India: All India Press, 1973).

9. J. Ehrenwald, "A neurophysiological model of psi phenomenon," *Journal of Nervous and Mental Diseases*, 154, 1972, 406-418.

10. K. Pribram, *Languages of the Brain*, (New York: Brandon House, 1971 1981).

11. L. G. Baranski, *The Frequency Spectrum and the Principle of Resonance Absorption*, North American Aviation, 1963.

12. U. Slager, *Space Medicine*, (Englewood Cliffs, NJ: Prentice-Hall, 1962).

CHAPTER 11

1. S. Chinmoy, *Kundalini: The Mother Power*, (Jamaica, NY: Agni Press, 1974).

2. H. Motoyama, "The Motoyama device: measuring psychic energy," in *Impact of Science on Society*, 24:4, 1974.

3. _____. "An electrophysiological study of Prana (Ki)."

4. H. Jenny, *Cymatics: Structure and Dynamics of Waves and Vibrations*, vol. I, (New York: Schocken, 1975).

CHAPTER 12

1. J. Campbell, "Seven levels of consciousness," in *Psychology Today*, December 1975, 77-78.

2. C.W. Leadbeater, *The Chakras*, (Wheaton, IL: Theosophical Publishing House, 1980).

3. S.Rama, R. Ballentine, and S. Ajaya, *Yoga and Psychotherapy: The Evolution of Consciousness*.

4. L. B. Fierman, *Effective Psychotherapy: The Contribution of Hellmuth Kaiser*, (New York: Free Press Division of Macmillan, 1965).

5. H. Motoyama, *Theories of the Chakras: Bridge to Higher Consciousness*, (Wheaton, IL: Theosophical Publishing House, 1981).

6. _____. *Science and the Evolution of Consciousness*, Brookline, MA: Autumn Press, 1978).

7. G. Murphy, *The Challenge of Psychical Research*, (New York: Harper-Colophon Books, 1961).

8. Ibid., p. 12.

9. G. G. Luce, *Biological Rhythms in Human and Animal Physiology*, (New York: Dover Publishers, 1971).

10. I. Jamal, "The magic of African medicine," *East West Journal*, 13:7, July 1983, 42-46.

CHAPTER 13

1. C. Whitaker and T. Malone, *The Roots of Psychotherapy*, (New York: Brunner/Mazel, 1981), p. 90.

CHAPTER 14

1. F. Capra, "The Tao of Physics Revisited," *Re-Vision*, 4:1, 1981, 36-52.

2. J. Trefil, *From Atoms to Quarks*, (New York: Scribners, 1980).

3. B. DeWitt, "Quantum mechanics and reality," *Physics Today*, 23:9, 1970, 30-35.

4. D. Bohm, *Wholeness and the Implicate Order*, (London: Routledge, Kegan Paul, 1980).

5. W. Scott, *Erwin Schrodinger: An Introduction to His Writings*, (Amherst: University of Massachusetts Press, 1967).

6. A. Rose, "Quantum Effects in Human Vision," in *Advances in Biological and Medical Physics*, vol. V, (New York: Academic Press, 1957).

7. W. Heisenberg, "Monitor," *New Scientist*. July 24, 1975, 196.

8. G. Hooft, "Gauge theories and the forces between elementary particles," *Scientific American*, 242:6, 1980.

9. D. Bohm, *Causality and Chance in Modern Physics*, (Philadelphia: University of Pennsylvania Press, 1957).

10. F. Capra, "The Bootstrap hypothesis," *Re-Vision*, 4:2, 1981.

11. G. F. Chew, "Bootstrap: A scientific idea?", *Science*, vol. 161, 1968, 762-765.

12. D. Bohm, *Wholeness and the Implicate Order*, p. 87.

CHAPTER 15

1. A. Einstein, B. Podolsky, and N. Rosen, "Can Quantum Mechanical Description of Reality Be Considered Complete?" *Physical Review*, vol. 47, 1935, 777.

2. J. Bell, "Quantum Interconnectedness," *Physics*, I, 1964, 195.

3. D. Bohm and B. J. Hiley, "On the intuitive understanding of nonlocality as implied by quantum theory," in *Foundations of Physics*, 5:1, March 1975.

4. J. Wheeler, *Geometrodynamics* (New York: Academic Press, 1962).

5. B. d'Espagnat, "The quantum theory and reality," *Scientific American*, 241:5, November 1979, 158-181.

6. G. Feinberg, "Possibly faster than light particles," *Physics Review*, 159, 1967, 1089.

7. D. Bohm and B. J. Hiley, "On the intuitive understanding of nonlocality."

8. A. Whitehead, *Process and Reality*, (Toronto: Macmillan Co., 1929).

9. E. Leith and J. Upatnieks, "Photography by laser," *Scientific American*, 212:6, June 1965.

10. D. Bohm, *Wholeness and the Implicate Order*, p. 172.

11. *Ibid.*, p. 149.

CHAPTER 16

1. S. Aurobindo, *The Life Divine*, (Pondicherry, India: All India Press, 1973), p. 524-25.

2. Ibid., p. 536.

3. Ibid., p. 544-45.

222 Notes for Chapter 16

222 Notes for Chapter 16

4. S. Rama, *Lectures on Yoga*, (Honesdale, PA: Himalayan International Institute Publishers, 1971).

5. S. Ajaya, *Yoga Psychology*, (Honesdale, PA: Himalayan International Institute Publishers, 1976).

6. K. Pribram, *Languages of the Brain*, (New York: Brandon House, Inc., 1971 1977), p. 73.

7. Y. Ramacharaka, *Fourteen Lessons in Yoga Philosophy and Oriental Occultism*, (Chicago: Yogi Publication Society, 1903).

8. H. Minkowski in A. Einstein, et al., *The Principle of Relativity* (New York: Dover, 1923), p. 75.

9. D. T. Suzuki in Preface to B. L. Suzuki, *Mahayana Buddhism* (London: Allen and Unwin, 1959), p. 8.

CHAPTER 17

1. J. Eccles, "The physiology of imagination," *Scientific American*, 199:3, 1958, 135-146.

2. E. R. John, R. N. Herrington, and S. Sutton, "Effects of visual form on the evoked response," *Science*, 155, 1967, 1439-42.

3. K. Pribram, "The neurophysiology of remembering," *Scientific American*, January 1969, 73-86.

4. K. Pribram, L. Kruger, F. Robinson, and A. Berman, "The effects of precentral lesions on the behavior of monkeys," *Yale Journal of Biology and Medicine*, 28, 1956, 423-443.

5. F. Campbell, G. Cooper, and Enroth-Cugell, "The spatial selectivity of the visual cells of the cat," *Journal of Physiology*, 203, 1969, 223-235.

6. Ibid.

7. D. A. Pollen, "How does the striate cortex begin the reconstruction of the visual world?" *Science*, 173, 1971, 74-77.

8. K. Pribram, *Languages of the Brain*, pp. 19-25.

9. E. Walker, "Quantum mechanical tunneling in synoptic and ephaptic transmission," *International Journal of Quantum Chemistry*, vol. 11, 1977, 103-127.

10. A. P. Dubrow, "Biogravitation and Psychotronics," in *Impact of Science on Society*, 24:4, 1974.

11. J. Hasted, *The Metal-Benders*, (London: Routledge, Kegan Paul, 1981).

12. K. Pribram and D. McGuiness, "Arousal, activation and effort in the control of attention," *Psychological Review*, vol. 82, 1975, 116-149.

CHAPTER 18

1. P. V. I. Khan, *Physics and the Alchemy of Consciousness*, (New Lebanon, NY: Sufi Order Publications, 1978), p. 12.

2. M. Cade and N. Coxhead, *The Awakened Mind: Biofeedback and the Development of Higher States of Awareness*, (New York: Dell Publishing, 1980).

3. K. Wilber, "Ontogenetic development: two fundamental patterns," *Journal of Transpersonal Psychology*, 13:1, 1981, 33-58.

4. E. Walker, "The nature of consciousness," *Mathematical Biosciences*, 7, 1970, 175-176.

5. E. P. Wigner, "The place of consciousness in modern physics," in E. Muses and A. Young, eds., *Consciousness and Reality*, (New York: Avon Books, 1974), pp. 132-141.

6. S. Aurobindo, *The Synthesis of Yoga*, (Pondecherry, India: Sri Aurobindo Ashram, 1981), p. 989.

7. S. Muktananda, *The Play of Consciousness*, (New York: Harper and Row, 1978), p. 265.

8. B. DeWitt, "Quantum mechanics and reality," *Physics Today*, 23:9, 1970, 30-35.

9. *Brain/Mind Bulletin*, issue on Multiple Personality, 8:16, Oct. 3, 1983.

10. W. Y. Evans-Wentz, *Tibetan Yoga and Secret Doctrines*, (London: Oxford University Press, 1958).

11. H. Benson, et al., "Body temperature changes during the practice of Tum-me yoga," *Nature*, vol. 295, January 1982, 234-235.

CHAPTER 19

1. A. S. Presman, *Electromagnetic Fields and Life*, (New York: Plenum Press, 1970).

2. Y. A. Kohlodov, "Effects on the central nervous system," in M. F. Barnothy, ed., *Biological Effects of Magnetic Fields*, vol. 1.

3. K. R. Pelletier, *Mind as Healer/Mind as Slayer* (New York: Dell Publishing Co., 1977), pp. 62-70, 134-139.

4. J. Hasted, *The Metal-Benders*.

5. B. Aaronson, "Hypnotic alternatives of space and time," *International Journal of Parapsychology*, 10, 1968, 5-36.

6. J. C. Pearce, "Role models and randomicity," Address delivered at the 7th International Transpersonal Psychology Conference, Bombay, India, Feb. 1982.

7. S. Vivekananda, *Raja Yoga*, (New York: Ramakrishna-Vivekananda Center, 1955), p. 151.

8. J. A. Wheeler, "From relativity to mutability," in J. Mehra, ed., *The Physicist's Conception of Nature*, (Dordrecht, Holland: Reidel Publishing Company, 1973), pp. 202-247.

CHAPTER 20

1. D. Kunz and E. Peper, "Fields and their clinical implications," I, II and III, *The American Theosophist*, December 1982 and January 1983.

2. S. Krippner, *Human Possibilities: Mind Exploration in the USSR and Eastern Europe*, (Garden City, NY: Anchor Press/Doubleday, 1980).

3. P. Russell, *The Global Brain: Speculations on the Evolutionary Leap to Planetary Consciousness*, (Los Angeles: J. P. Tarcher, 1983).

Glossary

Alayavijnana or Alaya. The all-conserving soul or mind of the Mahayana Buddhists in which the "germs" of all things in the external phenomenal world exist in their idealized state.

Archetype. The primordial energy-idea forms that express universal images and relationships which humankind has inherited from thousands of years of living together. They exist in the collective unconscious as outlined by C. G. Jung.

Biogravitational field. The intelligent energy field of the subtle body that is capable of transmitting affect and information from one organism to another.

Brainwaves. The four different kinds of electromagnetic waves produced by the human brain, measured in cycles per second (c.p.s.). Each is associated with a different state of consciousness; Beta, 12-20+ c.p.s. is the waking state; Alpha, 9-11 c.p.s., is calm relaxation and sometimes meditation; Theta, 5-8 c.p.s., is dreaming and/or reverie; Delta, 5-4 c.p.s., is deep dreamless sleep.

Chitta. Generally termed the memory or "mind-stuff" in yoga.

Holonomic flow or Holoflux. The flow of worlds within worlds or the idea that all is contained and reflected in each aspect of everything else.

Kundalini. The unmanifest potential energy in all things that remains in a dormant state until awakened, often referred to as the Serpent Power that sleeps coiled in humans at the base

225

of the spine. Its release leads to physiological, psychic, and spiritual metamorphosis.

Manas. Those parts or aspects of the mind that apprehend or take in the impressions of the external world; the sensory and intellectual gates of the mind.

Manomaya Kosha. The level of the Self system that deals with the "mental" phenomena of the world. It is experienced as a body or sheath in yogic science.

Pranamaya Kosha. The level of the Self system that deals with the "energy body" or subtle body. Yogic breathing techniques interface with this level or sheath.

Pratayahara. The technique of conscious sensory withdrawal from the external world and focusing on the inner state.

Samadhi. The state of subjectless, objectless, thought-free pure consciousness in yogic science; the dreamless sleep, turiya, or Liberation.

Savasana. The technique of profound conscious physical and mental relaxation.

Synchronicity. The acausal connection or meaningful coordination of mental and physical phenomena in the world.

Turiya. The transcendental fourth state of human consciousness; the state beyond waking, dreaming, and dreamless sleep.

Yoga Nidra. The technique of consciously entering and influencing the dream state with no break in continuity; similar to lucid dreaming.

Index

Ackerman, N., ix
acupuncture, 48
adrenergia, 70, 98, 115-19
Alayavijnana, 22, 32, 141
anger, 198-99
Aristotle, xv, 18
Aurobindo, S., 149-52, 175
autonomic nervous system, 44-45, 57-58, 68-70

biofeedback, 17, 44-45, 47-48, 90
biogravitational field, 50-52
bioplasma, 49, 104
Bohm, D., 134-35, 144, 177
Bolen, J. S., 94
borderline personality, 154-55, 174, 177
brain, 159-67, 175-76
brainwaves, 84-85, 161, 162; in meditation, 88-89; patterns, 159-60, 163-64
breathing techniques, 58. *See also Nadi shodhanam*
Burr, H., 46-47

causal body, 91, 188
causality, 96-97
chakras, 103; and family motifs, 108-112
character armor, 54

cholinergia, 70, 98, 115-19
clinical death, 16
cognitive styles, 74
collective unconscious, 8-9, 21, 22
complementarity, 131-32
consciousness, 126, 176; elevation of, 179-80; and energy, 113, 157; and fields, 89; and physics, 133-34; pure light of, 190; at quantum level, 165-67; states of, 188; and thought, 157, 171, 175
crisis telepathy, 71

Dean, D., 68
death, moment of, 16-17
DeBroglie, L., 138-39, 140, 146
dream interpretation, 29, 30; in families, 21, 36-38
dreaming, witness of. *See* Witness
dreams, 10, 28-34, 73, 83, 90; lucid, 85, 95; timelessness in, 10; *See also* Time
Dubrov, A., 50-51, 166-67
dynamics, patient-therapist, 120

ESP. *See* Psi
Eccles, J., 160, 163, 175

ego, 149, 152-53, 155-56;
    -awareness, 85-87, 202; ex-
    pansion of, 88
Ehrenwald, J., 76, 86
electromagnetic force, 182-84
elementary particles, 128-30,
    133-35
emotional coherence, 97-98
energy body, 55, 58
energy patterns. *See* Family
    Unconscious
energy shells, 101; and con-
    sciousness, 101-2

family, the, 74; interactional
    themes in, 108-112; as a
    system, 37
family therapy, x, 35-38
Family Unconscious, 10-14,
    20-22, 119-21, 167, 196-97;
    energy patterns in, 14, 51;
    interpenetration in, 153-54;
    resonance in, 98-99, 155,
    167; system of the, 7
field, Family Unconscious as a,
    44; of organisms, 52, 121;
    psyche as a, 98. *See also* Bio-
    gravitational Field, Life
    Field, Quantum Field
fields, emotional, 12; and in-
    formation, 138-39; inter-
    connectedness of, 140-42;
    and matter, 128
field theory, 12-13
forces, interaction of. *See* In-
    teraction of forces
formative causation, 18
Freud, S., 7-9, 28, 69, 77

Hasted, J., 20, 184
Heisenberg, W., 43, 66-67,
    132-35
Hilbert space, 176, 189

holographic or holonomic
    model, 143-45, 152, 163-65
hundredth monkey, 19-20
hypnosis, 17, 70

implicate order, 187
indeterminacy principle, 132
interaction of forces, 127-31,
    182-84, 208-9
Inyushin, U. M., 49, 104

Jackson, Don, ix
Jenny, H., 104
Jung, C. G., 8-9

knowledge, levels of, 149-52
Krippner, S., ix-xi, 45, 70, 75
Kunz, D., 198, 199

Life fields, 46-47, 48-49
light, wave or particle, 131, 138

Malone, T., 120
Mandukya Upanishad, 82, 89
Manomaya Kosha, 55, 101
many-worlds concept, 176,
    179, 189
McConnell, R. A., 67
McDougall, W., 18-19
meditation, affect on chakras,
    103; physiological effects,
    58, 90
memory, 163
mental-egoic aspect, 73, 174;
    experience, 22; system, 9
morphogenetic fields, 17-18
Motoyama, H., 103, 109
Muktananda, S., 176
multiple personality, 178-79

nadi shodhanam, 55-56
nonlocality, 19, 129, 142, 174
Northrup, F. S., 46

object-relations school, 154
observer, 185. *See also* Witness
Om, 104
open systems, psyche as, 75

paranoid personality, 177-78
participant observer, 67
passive attention, 102-3
Peper, E., 198, 199
personal unconscious, 8, 9-10
personality, the, 173, 174, 177
plexuses. *See Chakras*
pranayama, 58, 179
pranayama kosha, 54, 55, 101
pratayahara, 87, 103
preconscious, 8
Pribram, K., 144, 156, 160-64, 171, 175
primary process, 7, 10, 38, 71, 97, 119-20
psi, 65-72, 87, 115-21, 197, 201; in families, 95-96; and Family Unconscious, 75; and space-time, 69-70
psi dreams, 76, 77-81
psychology, models for, 126-127
psychotic insight, 5, 178

quantum field, 13, 128-30, 135, 139

Rama, S., 58, 90, 156
rapid eye movement (REM), 83-84
Reich, W., 54
Relativity, 13, 139, 141
relaxation, art of, 87
Rhine, J. B., 65-66, 77
Rhine, L., 66
Rolfing, 46

Savasana. See Relaxation, art of

Schmeidler, G. R., 67
Schrödinger, 131-32
Schwarz, B. E., 80-81
Self, 172-75, 177, 180, 185, 187, 191; and ego, 202; in family members, 200; in psi, 141
self-determination, 135
self-organization, xiii-xiv, 185-86
sheep-goat pattern, 67-68
Sheldrake, R., 17-18
sleep, 83-90; changes in, 97
sleep cycle, 83-85
space and time, 186-87; in dreams, 6, 28, 91; and ego, 172; in Family Unconscious, 139-41; theories of, 69, 145, 186-87, 189, 190, 204
space-time continuum, 134; events, 157, 169
Stekel, W., 69
store-consciousness. *See Alayavijnana*
Sushumna, 49
synaptic transfer, 165-66
synchronicity, 9, 94, 117

Tart, C., 69
telepathy, in families, x, 80-81. *See also* Crisis telepathy
thought-waves, 156
Tibetan Book of the Dead, 16, 190
time, in dreams, 79-81. *See also* Space and time
tunneling, 166-67
Turiya, 89, 188

Ullman, M., 92-93
unconscious, the, 7, 8, 21; not spatial, 76. *See also* Collective Unconscious, Family

Unconscious, Personal
Unconscious

Vivekananda, S., 189
Void, the (THAT), 190

Walker, E., 165-66
Watson, L., 19
Wheeler, J., 66, 140

Whitaker, C., 114, 120
witness, the, 171, 176; of
    dreaming, 90-91

yantra, 104n
Yoga Nidra, 83, 85, 86, 89-91

zero-point, 134-35